D1648558

WHAT PEOPLE ARE SAYING ABOUT

Stew Leonard: My Story

"Stew's book is wise, funny, uplifting and as feel-good as a banana split from an ice cream counter."

—A.E. Hotchner

"I had a bunch of meetings scheduled for yesterday afternoon. Then Stew's book arrived. I started reading it and got so engrossed in it that I cancelled my meetings and finished the entire book instead. I loved it!"

—Jim Perdue, CEO Perdue Farms

"Stew Leonard guides you through the history of his family company with insightful observations about managing your family and your business. He describes how to successfully grow and pass your company as well as how to discover the silver lining for obstacles in your path. This helpful book will inspire persistence and motivate you to pursue excellence."

—John A. Davis, Faculty Chair, Families in Business Program, Harvard Business School

"Stew is one of those remarkable people you are lucky to meet once in a lifetime. He created an unbelievable business that has professionals coming from all over the world to see how they do it. But Stew is far more than this. He has a level of adulation from his team members and customers which just has to be seen to be believed. But what makes Stew Leonard someone really special is the way he dealt with the difficult points in his life and bounced back. This book is a must read for anyone wanting to find out what the DNA is for success and how to overcome tough times."

—Graeme Alford, author *Never Give Up*

"Stew Leonard proves you can get knocked down and come back stronger and wiser. He gives an open and honest description of the highs and lows. I was definitely inspired. You will be too."

—Wally "Famous" Amos, entrepreneur and literacy advocate

"Stew Leonard's 'My Story' is a deeply moving and thought-provoking book. On the personal side, his insights on getting through exceedingly tough times with no self-pity are a gift with a lift to the human spirit. On the business side, Stew's reminders to S-Satisfy, build T-Teamwork, achieve E-Excellence and make the customer say W-Wow, are invaluable keys to success. This remarkable book will be my gift to our entire global team."

—Greg Anderson, Founder & CEO, The Cancer Recovery Foundation International Group of Charities and author of *Cancer: 50 Essential Things to Do*

"If ever a book had heart, this is it! While reading this remarkable book, you'll laugh a lot and maybe shed a tear or two. Most importantly you'll discover a treasure trove of unique and creative ideas. No wonder Stew Leonard's is consistently on Fortune Magazine's '100 Best Places to Work' list.'"

—Danny Cox, author, *Leadership When the Heat's On*

"Stew writes the way he talks. That is why, after Stew's speech at our International Dale Carnegie convention, Mrs. Carnegie said, 'My husband, Dale would have loved to have known Stew. Dale would have wanted to take him on tour with him.'"

—Cal Walker, Dale Carnegie sponsor, retired

"Stew Leonard became "Entrepreneur of The Year" and built a great business in much the same way that Vince Lombardi became a legendary coach and built Super Bowl championship teams. Both taught their teams how to become brilliant at the basics. This book is much, much more than an autobiography. It's a great story written by someone whose message contains the lessons of success and fulfillment with your family, in your career, in your business and in life. I love this book and you will too!"

—Michael LeBoeuf, author of *How to Win Customers and Keep Them for Life*

"Stew Leonard is a great American success story. This amazing book is about an amazing man, his philosophy and why thousands upon thousands of customers come to shop at 'The Rock' every week. Stew is a marquee name at the head of an all-star cast. We are all richer for his honesty, his generosity and his tenacity."

—John Hoover, PhD, *New York Times* Best Selling Author

"Stew Leonard's contribution to the Bradford merchants was outstanding. He gave us a new outlook on retail merchandising. I was happy to be a part of it."

—H.L. "Woody" Woodruff, friend and former general manager, the Bradford Era

"As a customer, seeing the success of your stores, I've always wanted to know how you did it. Now I know. I think the book gives new insights into how you WOW the customer and team members"

—Jan Krivosheiw-Wenz, DCH

"Your book will be like a Bible for us retail people--a fascinating story about a successful entrepreneur. It's a jewel!"

—Bill Hollis, owner Billy's Bakery

"I was mesmerized by the book and couldn't put it down. I am going to read it again. This time with a notepad."

—Glenn Paraskevin, entrepreneur

STEW LEONARD:
My Story

THIS BOOK IS DEDICATED
TO THE MEMORY OF MY GRANDSON,
STEWART LEONARD III

STEW LEONARD'S PORTION OF THE NET PROCEEDS FROM THIS BOOK WILL BE DONATED TO:

To learn more about the charities' mission to promote water safety please visit:

WWW.STEWIETHEDUCK.COM

STEW LEONARD: My Story

Stew Leonard

with Scotty Reiss

Colle & Co., Publishers

FIRST EDITION

ISBN 978-1-61539-347-3

Produced by bellbookandhandle.com

CONTENTS

INTRODUCTION

Our wine buyer recently came up to me and said, "Our largest wine distributor made a mistake on our invoice. He short-changed himself by charging us the current vintage price instead of the reserve price on a shipment of wine. All together, he made a mistake in our favor of $2,400. What do you want me to do?"

I didn't even have to think about it. I learned the hard way to always do the right thing. Throughout this book, as you read it, you'll see that doing the right thing has allowed me to build a $400 million business employing more than 2,500 people. Doing the wrong thing landed me in federal prison camp for forty-two months, jeopardized my customers' confidence in me, and damaged the very business that I spent my entire life building. Doing the wrong thing also caused my loved ones lots of pain and suffering.

Putting my story on paper has been difficult for me. Many people told me that I was crazy to write this book and dredge up the problems of the past. Yet, I had a burning desire to write my story, hoping that it might help others grasp the lessons that I learned the hard way. My hope is that in reading this book, my experiences will convince you that any time that you run into a situation where there is a right way and a wrong way to something, you always choose the right way.

When you're an entrepreneur, it might be tempting to skip a step or two, but if you do, you'll soon realize, like I did, that there is no shortcut to success. Business is a lot like football. When you break the rules, you get penalized.

So what did I tell my wine buyer? I told him to do the right thing. As it turned out, the wine distributor was amazed to find out that the error on our bill was not an isolated case. It was a system-wide computer error, and the distributor had been undercharging all of his customers. The wine distributor was grateful, and now the trusted relationship between our two companies—just like the value of doing the right thing—is worth far more than the small financial gain that seemed so great at first.

chapter one

✦

BRADFORD TO THE RESCUE

Usually at this time of year, I would be attending the Boston Seafood Show in Massachusetts. In fact, my son Stew Jr. told me that he went to the show last week. He was there with a few of our managers. He said he somehow got ahead of the rest of the group and was walking down an aisle carrying one of our Stew Leonard's shopping bags, when a fellow spotted it and asked, 'Do you work at Stew Leonard's?'"

"Stew smiled and said, 'Yes, I do.'"

"The guy said, 'I hear the father got sentenced for underreporting his income, and the son is now running the business. How's the kid doing, anyway?'"

"Stew couldn't resist the opportunity. He smiled and answered, 'He's doing a helluva job!' Then, with a big grin he added, 'In fact, some people say he's doing an even better job than his father!'"

"The fellow was really impressed. Stew was savoring the moment until suddenly one of the fellows in the group yelled to him, 'We've been looking all over for you, Stew!'"

The audience broke into laughter. For a minute I felt like I'd gone back five years in time, before the nightmare had begun.

The reason I was standing in front of this audience was not because I had been sentenced to fifty-two months in prison for underreporting my income, but because the prison's warden, Dennis Luther, felt that my experiences as a merchant and as a retailer might be helpful to these people, all merchants and businesspeople of Bradford, Pennsylvania. Long an industrial town with oil fields, refineries, and manufacturing plants, Bradford was having a difficult economic time. Jobs had dried up, leaving the local businesses to struggle with fewer customers and with competition from the Wal-mart in a neighboring town.

Woody Woodruff, the general manager of the town's newspaper, the *Bradford Era*, worked with the town's Economic Redevelopment Committee headed up by Ray McMahon, and they were looking for ideas to revitalize the town's economy. For help, they'd approached Luther, warden of McKean Federal Prison, one of the town's largest employers. Luther was known for his innovative thinking, and for his belief that inmates were there *as* punishment, not *for* punishment. He had become quite famous for running one of the most progressive prisons in the country. In addition to the main prison, which was a medium-security facility surrounded by electric fences and razor wire, he ran a minimum-security camp, a campus of cinderblock buildings and no fence. It was home to mostly white-collar, nonviolent felons. Many were building contractors, businessmen, lawyers, or even politicians who had gone astray of the law.

That I ended up in Dennis Luther's charge was more than just plain good luck. I had read of his successes several years earlier when he was featured in Tom Peters's book *Thriving on Chaos*. Luther had been acclaimed as one of the finest wardens in the country, and my judge had requested that I be sent to McKean.

Even so, it is still a prison camp, where residents are subjected to the demeaning tones and pettiness of the guards and the boredom and loneliness of being away from families. The days are filled with humbling routines: breakfast at the crack of dawn and dinner at 4 p.m., head count two or three times a day, and working at menial jobs. There is the humiliation of visitation. (Residents are body-searched and made to line up against the wall in front of all of the visitors for roll call.) Plastic utensils, plates, and cups are used in the mess hall. Sharing a 6 by 9-foot cube with another guy, called your "bunkie," and a bathroom with twenty-seven other guys. Wearing the same drab khaki shirt and pants day after day. The routine alone could break your spirit. But if you maintained a positive attitude, it wasn't that bad. Most inmates soon learned to conform and settled in to do their time.

Everyone at McKean was given a full-time job. Soon after I arrived, I was assigned along with a fellow inmate named Glenn to the training center, a large log–cabin–style building a few hundred yards from the main prison where the guards and managers had training sessions and meetings. We were to be training center orderlies, responsible for keeping the center spotless, from the bathrooms to the kitchen sink. The center was a pleasant place and it all seemed quite familiar—people coming in for meetings, being cordial to each other, asking about families or weekends, or discussing a baseball game—but it was constantly made very clear to the orderlies that we were only there to do our work.

The job was simple. Early every morning after breakfast, we'd report to the center and get to work mopping and polishing the floors, emptying the trash, and, frequently, washing the dishes from the previous night's meetings. Every job had to be done perfectly, and if it wasn't, a guard was always there to show you the right way to do it.

One day I was assigned the job of washing all the windows in the entire building. I didn't want to tell my boss that I had never washed windows before. Fortunately, another inmate showed me how. "A bucket of warm water, a little Windex, and a lot of elbow grease, and your windows will be spotless," he told me. I washed and polished all day long and produced spotless, gleaming windows. I proudly wrote home to my son Stew Jr., telling him I had learned to "do windows." He wrote back, "Gee, Dad, I didn't know that they have computers at McKean!"

I quickly learned to keep my head down and mouth shut, remembering what Helen Keller once said: "The best way out is always through." My goal was to do my work.

One day, about six months into my term, Warden Luther made the trip across the street from the main prison to the camp office and summoned me. At first I was apprehensive, but his kind manner quickly calmed me down. He explained that the merchants in Bradford had approached him for help with their business problems, and he wondered if I might be willing to talk to them. He suggested that I give a talk to the Bradford Chamber of Commerce here at the prison training center. His idea was for me to share my merchandising philosophy and any ideas that they might be able to use in their own businesses.

Would I be willing to give a talk? You bet! It would be an honor! That night, filled with enthusiasm, I sat in my cube and started writing out my ideas on a legal pad. I had been in just about every tough spot you could think of when I was starting my own business, and from each situation came a lesson about the best way to solve the problem. I started to jot them down, and before I knew it, I had pages and pages of ideas and stories to share with the audience.

It felt strange to be standing in front of this group in the very room I'd mopped so many times, with dishes on the table that I'd washed just that afternoon, giving a talk about how to succeed in business. It was August 1994, ten months into my sentence, and for the first time I was excited about something other than my family visiting! I was allowed to mingle a bit before speaking to the group, and Woody and Ray introduced me to many of the members of the group: Betty Chu, proprietor of a Chinese restaurant; Grant Orris, a jeweler; Howard Nickel, who owned a paint store; Brenda Ruth, who operated a bed-and-breakfast; Lester Brauser, who ran an outdoor outfitting company; and Robert Brest, the Methodist minister. After a short time, the audience took their seats. I had decided to break the ice with the story about Stew at the seafood show. Although they all knew why I was in prison, it was still a difficult thing for me to explain. But I hoped that if I opened with the 800-pound gorilla in the room, they would be receptive to the ideas and suggestions I had to offer.

chapter two

CARPE DIEM, ONE DIEM AT A TIME

It seemed like the end of the world, but it was just the beginning when my dad died. I was just twenty-one years old.

I had learned the dairy business at my father's side, along with my brothers, Leo and Jim, at Clover Farms Dairy in Norwalk, Connecticut. My father had started the dairy, delivering milk by horse and buggy, in the early 1920s, just after he married my mother. He grew his little dairy on Catherine Street into a very successful operation, surviving the Depression and building a good business with a few hundred loyal customers. Dad taught me at a very young age that if you take good care of your customers, they will take good care of your business—and its profits will be your reward.

As a kid, I often went along with my father on his morning route. I helped load the trucks, wash the bottles, and collect payment from customers. The early hours and physical work didn't appeal to my brothers, who soon decided that they weren't interested in the milk delivery business, but I idolized my dad and wanted to be just like him.

My father, though, wanted more for me than a future of delivering milk to customers at the crack of dawn. He insisted that like my brothers and sisters, I go to college. He convinced me to apply to the Radcliff Hicks School of Agriculture at the University of Connecticut to study dairy management, where I learned the fundamentals of the dairy and food business, from running a farm to operating a milk plant and making ice cream. One of my professors, Leonard Dowd, was revered in the industry. I was always impressed when the owners and managers of large dairies sought his advice, and I was puzzled that he seemed so happy with his academic career. He could have had his choice of dairies anywhere in the country to run, and he probably would have made a lot more money. One day I asked him why he chose to be a college professor instead.

"I love teaching, Mr. Leonard, and doing what you love is much more important than making money." he replied. For the first time, I knew that I would be happy making a career of the milk business and working with Dad at the dairy: I loved what I did, too.

The university was located in Storrs, about two and a half hours from Norwalk. During the school year, I came home on weekends and holidays and worked at the dairy, giving the regular milkmen their days off; I also worked there during summer vacations. After graduating, I returned to the dairy full time. My brother Jim, who had enlisted in the Army and fought in World War II, had come home, too, and although his heart wasn't in it, my father convinced him to come work at the dairy. Jim and I took milk routes and joined the ranks of the milkmen.

When we suddenly lost our father due to a heart attack, the job of running the dairy fell on Jim and me. Stepping into our father's shoes meant taking on the responsibility of managing the business that supported the seven men who had worked for him for so long, the business that also sup-

My brother Jim (right), my mother, and I became owners of Clover Farms Dairy after my father died. I was just twenty-one years old.

ported our mother. But my father had prepared me for my future at the dairy, so I gathered my strength and resolved to make it work.

Part of that strength came from my brother Leo. He was the most brilliant person I have ever known, and Jim and I were lucky to have him nearby and willing to counsel us. Leo had followed his interest in engineering and attended the Massachusetts Institute of Technology, and after a career in the Navy designing shipyards, he returned home to start his own land surveying business. Although he didn't work at the dairy, Leo was our advisor and my mentor, and he took me under his wing. Jim and I rarely made a decision without first running it by Leo. As close brothers, we soon settled into a comfortable division of labor: Jim preferred supervising the morning milk routes and making deliveries, which left his afternoons free for sailing. I took over the office and dairy operations.

My biggest challenge in the early days was with the men. At first I tried to imitate my father's stern style of giving orders, which had always worked for him, but they almost mutinied. These men had worked for my father longer than I had been alive. My experience and my college education meant nothing to them. They resented taking orders from me. The more they ignored me, the more frustrated I became. I couldn't understand what I was doing wrong.

Managers say, "Go." Leaders say, "Let's go!"

Seeing my frustration—and fearing that a revolt would sink the dairy permanently—Leo stopped by my office one day.

"You might want to read this. It may help you manage your men." He handed me a copy of *How to Win Friends and Influence People* by Dale Carnegie.

I went home that night and began to read it. I couldn't put it down. After I finished the book, I wanted more. I called the Dale Carnegie office in New York and learned that Bob Stroud would soon be conducting a class at the Stamford Hotel in Stamford, Connecticut. My enthusiasm even inspired a few friends to come along with me: John, Tommy, and Jimmy Gardella; Bob Andre; and Sam Deorie. We were like sponges, soaking up all that the Dale Carnegie method had to offer.

The method taught us the fundamental principles of human relations: to think in terms of the other person's interests, to avoid being critical, and to show honest, sincere appreciation. "Develop these abilities and you will be able to lead other people and win them to your way of thinking. You will be able to convince the other person to do what you want them to do, because they will want to do it," we were taught.

When I learned Dale Carnegie's first two rules—"Don't criticize, condemn, or complain," and "Give honest, sincere appreciation"—I thought I had discovered magic. After practicing this new approach in class, I was eager to use it to turn my most difficult critics into friends. Back at the dairy, I approached Ray Flewellyn, who had been my father's right-hand man for almost thirty years. I started by complimenting him on our "cream line," thanking him for the good job he was doing getting the perfect balance of milk at the bottom of the bottles and cream at the top of the bottles, which had often been a problem. As I praised his talents, I felt him warm up to me. From then on, I was sure to keep up the praise for every job well done. And Ray soon began to bring me ideas and suggestions for improving operations.

When I saw how well the Dale Carnegie technique worked with Ray, I began to use it with all the men. I looked for things to applaud, for compliments to give. Eventually, I sometimes even offered praise when it wasn't deserved. It wasn't long before the men caught on, and they started calling me "Dale" in a negative way. I realized that I had forgotten the two most important words from the Dale Carnegie method: *honest* and *sincere*. I'd overdone it, and my efforts had backfired.

I became determined to master the Dale Carnegie principles and not simply exercise its basic tenets for my benefit, so I enrolled in the course again. I learned to change not just my tone and my words, but my way of thinking, my way of seeing things, and the approach I took with each problem and each man on our team. Slowly my results began to improve. Dale Carnegie's methods were changing my life.

The Iceman Cometh and Go-eth Away

A few years after our father died, Jim decided he'd had enough of the dairy business. He wanted to move his family to Florida, buy a catamaran, and offer cruises around the Keys. Leo, Jim, and I came up with an agreement: we would settle on a price, I would buy Jim's share, and Jim would take payment in monthly installments. Unfortunately, Jim wasn't the only one who was tiring of the dairy home delivery business—customers were, too. They liked picking up their milk at the supermarket and saving money. Small dairies were selling out to larger ones, and supermarkets were popping up around town offering lower prices on milk and other dairy products.

To combat the new competition, I began a marketing campaign like no other. We installed animated cows' heads on top of our trucks and rigged the horns to "moo." We painted a message on the sides of the trucks, "You Wave and I'll Moo!" We sponsored competitions and sporting events at the high school. To get our milkmen to sign up new customers, we held contests that awarded them TV sets or trips to Bermuda. We offered discounts to customers and installed milk vending machines at the dairy that allowed them to buy their milk at lower prices than the supermarkets offered, at any hour of the day or night. Still, that first year after Jim left the dairy, sales dropped 12 percent.

Despite the drop in sales, Leo and I believed we could survive.

"Just be the best," Leo advised. "People will always want the convenience of having fresh milk delivered to their doorstep." I agreed.

We believed that we always produced the freshest, best-tasting milk in town, and to sell that point, we built an image around the slogan "You'd Have to Own a Cow to Get Fresher Milk." Then a friend, Jack Goerhing, introduced me to Joe Shaw, a former advertising agency art director in New York City. Joe had worked on big national campaigns including Revlon, but had tired of the commute to New York City and the stress of the agency business, so he retired early and built an art director's studio behind his home. He took me under his wing and encouraged me to promote our "farm fresh" image. We changed our newspaper ads, and put new signs on everything from the sides of our trucks to the side of our dairy. Joe's vision was to build Clover Farms Dairy into a brand, using ads promoting the freshness of our products by featuring cows in a field near the dairy. (Our calendar even featured my daughter Jill sitting on a Holstein's back.)

Joe Shaw's marketing methods stabilized our business, but other dairies around New England were finding different solutions to the changing economy. One day Gene Devine, whose small family dairy, with its beautiful buildings and pristine bottling operation, delivered milk to neighboring towns, told me that he had decided to sell his dairy.

"It's a dying business," Gene told me. "The milkman is going the way of the iceman." I refused to believe him.

Bulldozers break ground after the state of Connecticut decided to build a highway right through the center of our property.

People didn't need ice deliveries anymore because they had modern refrigerators and freezers, but I thought the convenience of milk delivery would remain a necessity. People would always want fresh milk, just as Leo had said. So I purchased Devine Dairy, which doubled my sales. I had to build an addition onto the dairy to garage the extra delivery trucks. Even though the industry was shrinking, we seemed to be doing fine. I was sure we could survive.

Then one day Leo burst into my office with a roll of maps under his arm and alarm in his voice. "The state of Connecticut is going to build a highway right through the middle of the dairy. They are going to put you out of business!"

Leo unrolled the maps on the desk, showing me the plans for the extension of Route 7, which would cut right through the middle of our processing plant. I was stunned.

"The state will use their power of eminent domain to condemn your property. There is no use trying to fight their plans," Leo said. It would be expensive to fight the state in any case, and I didn't have a lot of money for a legal battle. I wondered if I might be the one to close the family business that my father had built.

Eventually I came to the conclusion that the state's plan might be an opportunity for me to move to a bigger property and expand my business. More and more households were choosing less-expensive supermarket milk over home delivery, but if I could add some wholesale customers, we might be able to grow. My dream included a gleaming state-of-the-art processing plant, modern new buildings, and a streamlined bottling plant. I met with Robert Johnson of Hertel Johnson Eipper & Stopa, an architectural firm in Chicago that designed and built modern dairies. He came to Norwalk, toured our dairy with me, and listened to my plans for expansion. Then he gave me his opinion.

"I'm sorry, Stew, we just don't build little dairies like yours anymore," he said. Modern automated dairy plants needed substantial volume, much more than I could supply even if I successfully expanded my business.

I was forced to rethink my plan.

When Life Gives You Lemons—Build a Lemonade Stand!

I began to look everywhere I could for ideas. I visited dairies up and down the East Coast, from Massachusetts to Florida. One day my friend Mort Perry, who owned the Pickwick Ice Cream Company in Stamford, dropped by. I explained my problem and he suggested I take a drive with him to Long Island to see one of his best customers, Gouz Dairy. When Bernie Gouz and his brother Willie had been in a situation similar to mine, they created a retail milk store and discontinued their home delivery routes. They sold freshly bottled milk right from their dairy at cheaper prices than the supermarkets, as well as ice cream, bread, eggs, and juice.

That Saturday, Mort and I drove to Long Island. As we neared Bernie's store, traffic slowed to a crawl. Soon I realized that we weren't in any ordinary traffic jam, we were in the line to get into the Gouz Dairy parking lot! A huge sign on the front of the building read "Gouz Rhymes with COWS," and underneath, it said, "MILK: 22 Cents a Quart." I couldn't believe my eyes. Customers were streaming into an old dairy barn—the Gouz store—and coming out with wire carriers loaded with quart glass bottles of milk, armloads of bread, and large boxes of eggs. It was a sensation!

I was immediately impressed by the Gouz operation and realized that I might have discovered the solution to my problem here. Mort introduced me to Bernie, and we became friends right away. His generosity amazed me.

Flattered that I wanted to imitate his store, Bernie kindly offered any advice he could give. I had what seemed like a thousand questions, and as Bernie answered them, I became more and more excited.

I went back to Norwalk filled with enthusiasm, and I called Joe Shaw. I had a good idea of just want I wanted in a retail store, but I had to find the right architect to design it. Joe introduced me to his neighbor, a young architect named Dick Bergmann. The more Dick, Joe, and I talked about it, the more we could see our new store in our minds: a classic dairy barn with a silo and a pitched roof, with modern facilities and beautiful stainless-steel processing tanks inside.

Dick Bergmann and me at the site of the new dairy store.

Then Dick asked me the one question I couldn't answer: where, exactly, was the store going to be located?

I had gotten ahead of myself. I had been so focused on finding the right idea that I hadn't thought about finding the right place to build it. I began to comb the busy roads in town looking for vacant property and one day I found it: a small farm on Route 1 in Norwalk. It was perfect. More than 16,000 cars passed by each day. That wasn't just 16,000 cars, that was 16,000 potential customers! I excitedly brought Leo to see this great location I'd found.

"Forget it," Leo said. "It isn't for sale." He knew that the farm was owned by Hazel Schultze, a widow who'd had offers on the land from everywhere from Norwalk to New York, and she always refused to sell. But Mrs. Schultze had been a customer of my father's, so I approached her anyway, and she even remembered me! I soon discovered that one of the reasons she didn't want to sell her land was that she was concerned about her sheep that grazed the land, the chickens in her yard, and the hired hand who took care of them for her, George Blanarik. She didn't want to displace any of them. After a few conversations and a lot of listening, Mrs. Schultze agreed to sell me one and three-quarter acres of her pasture as long as I also agreed to buy her animals and to hire George to take care of them. It wasn't a hard sell; I would build a little farm in front of our new dairy store.

With the problems of how to market my milk and where to relocate my dairy solved, I was left with only one last mountain to climb: money. The state of Connecticut paid

My brother Leo, our attorney Tom Flaherty, and I survey the property for our new dairy store on Westport Avenue.

us $208,000 for our property, but after I settled with the attorneys and paid off our mortgages, there was only $90,000 left, not nearly enough to build a new dairy store. My uncle Tom Stewart, who had agreed to be our building contractor, explained that by the time we had poured the foundation for the new store, the building costs, which I had estimated would be around $130,000, would be more than $500,000, and that wouldn't include the mortgage payments to Mrs. Schultze or the new processing equipment, display cases, refrigeration, and registers.

To get the extra money, my wife, Marianne, and I scraped together every penny we could, took a second mortgage on our house, and even borrowed against the children's little

Boston Whaler boat that we used for fishing and waterskiing in the summer. But it still wasn't enough.

My friend Phil Baker suggested I call the Small Business Administration. After filing what seemed like a mountain of paperwork, my friend and attorney Tom Flaherty called one day to announce that our loan had been approved. We received a loan from Merchants Bank and Trust that was guaranteed by the SBA. I was sure it would be enough.

But it wasn't. Even though our store looked like a barn, I insisted on using only high-quality materials, because I believe that the cheapest in the short run is the most expensive in the long run. We spared no expense on the new building, inside and out. We installed automatic front doors and put in coolers that had "air curtains" to keep the cold air inside but allowed customers to easily reach in for the products they wanted. We bought shiny new stainless-steel equipment, and glass windows framed our bottling plant so customers could see their milk being bottled. Ceramic tiles lined the walls, and hand-split cedar shakes covered the roof. I even had the front sidewalk heated so customers wouldn't slip on the ice in the winter; the snow would just melt away.

One evening, my accountant, Bill Kolkmeyer, stopped by with some bad news. We were over budget and the bills were still coming in. We had spent more than a million dollars, and we were running out of money. He felt that we wouldn't have enough to finish the building. "You're $100,000 over budget already," Bill said, "and you're only three-quarters done."

To make matters worse, everyone I shared my plans with thought I was crazy. Sam Lang, who supplied our milk cartons and cases, thought our new store looked as nice as someone's home. "You're going to pay for all this selling only seven dairy items? You're out of your mind!" Chris Knudsen, a friend who owned Knudsen Dairy, one of the largest and most successful dairies in the state, said, "You must know something about the milk business that I don't."

That night I was unable to sleep. I went downstairs, took out a pad of paper, sat at the kitchen table, and began making one list of why I could succeed and another list of why I might fail. The fail list was much longer. I thought of my four children and my wife sleeping upstairs, and I felt like a failure. Soon the sun came up and Marianne came downstairs to make breakfast, and she was surprised to find me sitting there.

"What's the matter, Stew?" she asked.

"It doesn't look like we are going to make it," I said, and I read her my two lists. It was the first time I'd mentioned my fears of failure to her, and I poured out my heart. I told her of the predictions of failure, the naysayers who all said I was crazy, and the fact that we were running out of money.

To my surprise, she smiled. "Don't listen to those negative people, Stew. Stew, they're the ones who are crazy," she said. "Of course you'll succeed!" She went to the kitchen drawer and pulled out her savings passbook from the Norwalk Saving Society. She handed it to me.

"Here, you can use this. I've been saving it for the children's college fund, but you can put it back after the dairy is a success." The passbook showed a deposit of $3,300, money that Marianne had received as restitution from the German government for her parents' losses during World War II. I got up and gave her a hug.

I didn't have the heart to tell her that we needed a hundred thousand dollars!

But Marianne's faith and belief in me sparked a new energy, and I decided right then and there never to let anyone make me think negatively again. My motto was going to be "Don't walk away from negative people … run!"

With renewed enthusiasm, I set out on a selling campaign. I talked to every supplier and creditor I had, taking them on tours of the new dairy to show them the progress we were making, showing them our plans, and showing them our house and even the children's boat we'd lose if the store failed. I explained that I had everything we owned in the world on the line, and I needed their help. Fortunately for me, they all believed in me and agreed to extend my credit. Soon opening day was in sight.

Build It, and They Will Come—We Hope!

We worked night and day to get the store ready to open. We stressed our "Fresh from the Farm" image in everything we did. Our little farm, where we kept Mrs. Schultze's sheep and chickens, along with a few of our calves, would be fun for children who visited the store, and it would add to the overall farm feeling.

On Thanksgiving weekend, we were working around the clock to get the store ready for our grand opening, just a few days away. Marianne, our children, Stew Jr., Tom, Beth, and Jill, and our seven employees—former Clover Farms dairymen who had made the transition to processing the milk, running the new automated processing plant, and stocking the coolers—spent Thanksgiving Day helping out in the store. When a few customers came to the vending machines in the parking lot for a last-minute half-gallon of milk, they saw that the lights were on, and out of curiosity, some came inside to ask if we were open.

Not wanting to turn customers away, Stew pulled milk cartons off the conveyor belt and Jill hopped up on a milk crate and rang up the few customers, and we happily sent them on to their holiday dinners. We were elated that people were excited about coming into our new store; it was a good omen for our grand opening.

Finally, opening day arrived: November 30, 1969. It was the day before my fortieth birthday. We hung a sign in the window that said "Open." We watched as customers pulled into the parking lot, went directly to the vending machines, bought milk, and then drove away. I understood that they must not have realized that the store was open, so I quickly scribbled "Out of Order" on several slips of cardboard, ran across the parking lot, and taped the signs to the machines.

Soon people were coming inside for milk. They were

Opening day: November 30, 1969

happy to find eggs, bread, and ice cream, too. Children gazed through the window that looked into the bottling plant, pressing their noses against the glass to watch as the cartons were filled and made their way down the conveyor belt. They were delighted by the animals in our little farm. Parents quickly found they were making a trip to Clover Farms Dairy store not only because we had the freshest, best-priced milk in town, but also because their children loved the store. I soon learned that where children want to go, mothers follow.

Even with the store overflowing with customers, though, my profit margin was thin; it was a struggle to make each month's mortgage payments. The day before the 4th of July, 1970, a tractor-trailer pulled into our parking lot. The driver

Top: The store had one aisle, two cash registers, and a big picture window (left) that looked into our dairy plant.

Bottom: Our in-store dairy plant drew spectators—in the store and on the balcony that overlooked it.

had a load of watermelons fresh from South Carolina, he said, but his local order had fallen through; would I like to buy a few? I asked the price and he told me that watermelons were retailing for $5 apiece, but his wholesale price was only $2 each. I asked how many he had: 2,000. I offered to buy his entire truckload if he'd let me have them for $1 each.

"No way!" he said, and bolted out of the store. About half an hour later, he was back. He said he'd thought it over and would agree to my price if we unloaded the watermelons ourselves. He opened up the back doors of the truck, and there were the watermelons, packed neatly in straw from floor to ceiling.

"Would you park your trailer on our front sidewalk," I asked him, "and leave it there over the weekend?" He agreed.

First we hung a huge banner on the side of the truck, "Watermelons, $1 each. Limit 3 to a customer." Then we set up a cashier's table next to the truck and a couple of stock boys climbed up in the truck to hand out the watermelons. Customers crowded around the truck—you'd have thought we were giving them away! Bill Kolkmeyer saw the excitement as he drove by the store, and he stopped in. "How much did you pay for those watermelons, Stew?" he asked. When I told him, he thought I was crazy.

"You can't buy them for a dollar apiece and sell them for the same price! Do you know how much money you're losing?"

"I know, Bill, but look!" I pointed to the store's front

door. "All those customers are going in the store and buying lots of other things, too!" That weekend our sales tripled. True, we lost money on the watermelons, but we sold lots of milk, bread, and ice cream. By having a great deal on something customers wanted, we increased our sales on everything else.

And having the truck pulled up to our front door, filled with straw and fresh watermelons, gave me another idea: we could extend our "Fresh from the Farm" image to more than just dairy products. We soon started talking to local farmers, and before we knew it, we had trailer-truckloads of potatoes, corn, tomatoes, apples—anything I could find

Our first lesson in loss leaders: watermelons.

that we could buy straight from the farm and sell from the truck. We became living proof of the claim "We cut out the middleman and pass the savings on to customers." We even had to build special unloading bays for the trucks and new displays in the store. Before we knew it, our store and parking lot became even more crowded, and sometimes customers had to wait in line to get into the store.

An Offer I Could Refuse

One day in 1972, as I was building a bread display in the store, a couple of fellows in business suits approached me, introduced themselves, and asked to speak with me. I took them up the circular staircase in the silo to our offices, where we could sit and talk comfortably. The two men said they were Harvard Business School graduates and they'd been studying my store. They'd even done a case study of us by interviewing our suppliers, counting the customers in our parking lot, looking at our products and prices, and estimating our costs and revenues. They wanted to build a store just like ours. A whole group of stores, in fact. They had spreadsheets with one-year, five-year and ten-year business plans. They offered me the chance to join them in their new business. If I declined, they said, they would open stores like mine anyway, without my help.

They seemed like nice guys, but I had all I could do to run my own store. I couldn't possibly think about opening another store or even being a consultant to someone else.

Besides, my vision had always been to simply focus on freshness and take care of the customer. I believed that by sticking to those two philosophies, we would eventually have a rock-solid foundation under our business. A second store or a chain of stores was not part of my dream.

I told the fellows thanks anyway and wished them luck. I was flattered that they wanted to imitate my store, and I offered to give them any advice I could, just as Bernie Gouz had done for me. They took me up on my offer and over the months, stopped by with questions, seeking advice.

They had found a location in Milford, twenty miles away, and began building their store, called Millpond Farms. Apparently they were serious about replicating my store; customers who had driven by and seen the construction asked me, "Stew, when are you opening your new store in Milford?"

One day I decided to stop by and see for myself. I was stunned: the fellows had built a store that looked exactly like mine, from the silo to the cedar-shake roofing to the animal farm out front. They'd installed a dairy plant in the middle of the store and even the milk cartons and shopping bags were similar to ours. When I got back to the store, I called my attorney, Tom Flaherty, and asked if they could do this. His answer was, yes, they could. They could copy every detail, down to my name, Clover Farms Dairy, if they wanted to. Tom explained that since my father had never registered a trademark on the name, we didn't own it. A trademark was something I'd never even considered. If we wanted to

In 1972, "Stew Leonard's" became part of our store's name

protect our name, Tom said, we should find a name that would be uniquely ours that we could trademark. I went back to the store and called my brother Jim in Florida to get his advice. His answer was simple: the name that was most uniquely mine was Stew Leonard.

I hung up the phone and thought about what my father's reaction might be to changing the dairy's name to Stew Leonard's. I could almost hear him say, "What in the world are you doing, Stewart?" He'd chosen the name Clover Farms Dairy so many years ago and built it into the business that he passed on to his sons. I wondered if Dad would think it egotistical to put my name on the dairy. But my name was the only thing that no one could take from me, and it was something that I could pass on to my children. That, I knew, Dad would understand.

After a while, I sat down and began to carve my name into a plank of wood. When I finished, I hung the sign on the front of the store. That day, we became Stew Leonard's Clover Farms Dairy.

Pile 'em High, Watch 'em Buy!

One day, Leo took me to lunch at our favorite restaurant, Porky Manero's Steak House. On the way to our table, we passed a friend of his, a local lawyer and former probate judge named Bill Keene. Bill nodded hello, then stopped us.

"Your neighbor Hazel Schultze just died, and I am the executor of her estate," he said. "Perhaps you'd like to make an offer on her property. I might possibly even be able to arrange some easy terms for you." It was the solution to my biggest problem: how to expand my store so I could increase my selling space and my sales. With Mrs. Schultze's land, I could add on to the store. I jumped at the opportunity, even though I didn't know how I would be able to pay for my expansion dreams.

We had become known for our low prices and high-quality

dairy products and produce. I was able to offer better prices than the supermarkets because we either made the products ourselves or bought directly from local farmers, eliminating wholesalers and middlemen. I believed the same concept could work with national manufacturers, and it became my goal to bring in national brands at the same low prices.

With the addition to the store, I could stock more products. I began to buy from companies and manufacturers as far away as California, where we got our produce in the winter. I discovered that as long as I was willing to buy an entire trailer-truckload of a single item, I could purchase anything at rock-bottom prices. But since my warehouse wasn't big enough to stock a broad range of brands and sizes, the way the supermarkets did, I decided to sell only the top brand of each item: the best nationally advertised brand of tuna fish, the top brand of paper towels, the top brand of mayonnaise. Each of our products had to be the leader in its category. Then, in turn, I passed the savings on to the customer with "truck load specials," and customers were able to buy their favorite brands at lower prices than they could at the local supermarket. Through word of mouth, we became known for our "Buy Two, Get One Free" deals that offered even lower prices on every single item that we sold. One of our slogans became "We Lower the Price and Sell the Best, Word of Mouth Does the Rest."

Soon I also discovered that the bigger our displays were, the more we sold. And the more we sold, the more we could reduce the price for our customers, because the more we lowered our prices, the more truckloads we had to buy, enabling us to purchase at even better prices. Our strategy became "Pile 'em High, Watch 'em Buy."

While the supermarkets around town were having weekly sales with a few cents off on items that were "on special," we were able to offer everyday low prices on everything we sold. I soon realized I'd rather make 20 nickels than 4 quarters anytime!

One day, a friend who owned a supermarket in Minneapolis came to visit our store. As I showed him around, we came to a giant display of Bumble Bee tuna fish with a big sign that read "Tuna Fish $1.29 a Can/6 Cans for $5."

"Stew, what's your secret? How can you sell tuna at less than a dollar a can? Why, that's below wholesale!"

"Henry," I said, "my secret is simple: we buy below wholesale!"

Most supermarkets have a traditional retail floor plan: produce at the beginning, bakery at the end, cans and packaged goods in the center, and refrigerated cases and service counters along the back and side walls. (The cases and counters work best along the walls because they can be serviced from the back.)

But when I opened my little Clover Farms Dairy store, our layout was a simple U shape with refrigerated "coffin-style" ice cream cases in the middle of the U and refrigerated cases and bread racks around the perimeter. This meant that our store was essentially a single aisle with customers entering and leaving the same spot. But when we expanded the front of the store to give us more register space, our aisles were suddenly shaped like a T, which caused traffic jams and confusion. So we put more freezer cases in the center of store, again creating a center aisle. As we continued to expand the store, we followed the same concept of winding the aisle through the store, ultimately ending up with a labyrinth that leads from the front entrance to the cash registers.

We quickly realized that the labyrinth gave us two unique benefits: our customers had the opportunity to see every single product we sold, and the single aisle helped us to keep our selection limited to the items that our customers need most—we didn't have room to add more.

Eventually we saw another benefit to the single aisle: it allowed us to create a stage for freshness. Putting our production and packaging operations right in the center of the store meant our customers could see the freshness with their own eyes. The end result was another WOW! for the customer: the floor plan of our store created a sense of excitement and activity, and customers loved it.

By 1981, we carried 500 different items, we had twenty cash registers, and there were 300 Team Members. I was filled with bright ideas, and never in a million years did I think that my next bright idea would send me to a federal prison camp.

chapter three

TO KNOW THE ROAD UP THE MOUNTAIN, ASK SOMEONE WHO'S ALREADY BEEN TO THE TOP

Speaking to the Bradford merchants, standing there before a roomful of friendly people, all searching for ideas and solutions—anything that would help them with their struggling businesses—I was filled with a desire to help in any way that I could. Dwindling numbers of Bradford shoppers were passing by the small mom-and-pop operations. Local restaurants and inns had seen business decline, and even the Methodist church was concerned about attendance. The business community was looking for ways to create excitement and give people reasons to come back.

As I stood before the group, grateful for the opportunity to be out of my confining daily routine, I was hopeful that I could offer them suggestions and assistance, but I was not at all confident about how they might react. Although my presentation was ready, and my friend Glenn had the slide projector all set up, here I was, in prison-issue khakis, about to give my suggestions to the members of the Bradford Chamber of Commerce.

Telling the seafood show story seemed to break the ice. Now I could move on to the real reason I was standing here in front of this group.

"As you know, being an entrepreneur requires a lot of creativity," I said. "Well, I'm afraid I got carried away with my entrepreneurship. In fact, every day I hear a little voice in the back of my head saying, 'Boy, am I ever sorry for the dumb thing that I did. I sure had to learn my lesson the hard way!' Fortunately for me, every day I also hear another voice, and it's my mother's, saying, 'Remember, Stewart, life is 10 percent what happens to you and 90 percent how you react to it.' Being a dairyman, I know she's right—there's no use crying over spilled milk!"

As I stood there in the training center in front of this large group of shop owners and local business people, I began to feel like my old self again, the milkman who had become a successful business owner. For a moment I was able to forget where I was and why, and to focus on what it was that I could share with them about my experience that might help them through their difficult times.

I held up a copy of *In Search of Excellence* for the audience to see.

"I have a good friend, Tom Peters, who is the co-author of this famous business classic. When I told him I was coming here to Camp McKean, he said, 'You're lucky, Stew.' He told me he'd studied McKean when he was writing his latest book, *Liberation Management*. In fact, he had written a whole chapter praising Warden Dennis Luther's management style, and he knew Luther personally. He felt Luther was hands down the finest warden in the country! Tom said if given the choice, he'd rather be at McKean than any place else in the entire U.S. Bureau of Prisons system.

"I said, 'Maybe so, Tom, but if given the choice, I'd rather be back at my dairy store in Norwalk, Connecticut!'"

I wasn't sure that the audience knew anything about me or my store, so I filled in the blanks for them: I told them about my start as a milkman, the state's takeover of our dairy property, the demise of the home delivery milk business and my realization that, if I was going to survive, I'd have to change my marketing approach. I shared my dream with them: building a store with a dairy plant inside, a store that looked like a barn and even had a silo. I told them that one of my first slogans was "You'd Have to Own a Cow to Get Fresher Milk." I knew I could save my customers money because I cut out the middleman—me, the milkman! I told them about the naysayers who told me I was crazy to think that shoppers would pass by the dairy counters at their local supermarkets and make a special stop at my store just for their milk. Over the twenty-five years since opening day in November 1969, our customers have taught me what I call four simple secrets. I shared those secrets with the audience that day.

Secret 1. Satisfy Your Customers

I learned this the hard way. Two weeks after we opened, I was standing at the front door of our store proud as punch, greeting customers like a maître d' in a restaurant. A lady came up to me and said, "Your eggnog is sour!" and she thrust a half-gallon carton at me. My pride was hurt. "Eggnog from my brand new dairy, sour? No way!!" I said. And then I uttered two words I would soon regret: "You're wrong!" I told her. "We've sold over 200 cartons of eggnog from this batch, and you're the only one who's complained!" The lady was so angry that the veins were popping out in her neck. She said, "I don't care how many you've sold, it's sour and I want my money back!" Eggnog was 95 cents, so I reached into my pocket and gave her a dollar. She snatched it out of my hand and started out the door—she didn't even give me my nickel change. The last words I heard her say were, "I'm never coming back to this store again!"

That night, when I told Marianne the story she too, became upset with me. She said, "I don't blame her at all. She wasn't the one who was wrong, you were. You didn't listen to her. You contradicted her and you practically called her a liar. I hope you're not going to run your store like some store managers, who think all customers are trying to put something over on them. They don't trust us. But we fix them—we just never go back to that store again."

Marianne's words were like a bombshell: everything we had in the world was tied up in our store. I couldn't afford to lose a single customer by telling them they were wrong. Marianne was right, and I was the one who was wrong.

On my way to work each morning, I drove by Bate's Monument Yard, where huge slabs of granite were carved into gravestones. One morning I saw the workers unloading a huge rock, and I got an idea. I stopped and bought it. It was six feet tall and weighed 6,000 pounds. I had Mr. Bates deliver it to the front door of our store, and right there, in front of customers and our Team Members, a stonemason chiseled our new policy into its face:

Rule 1 The Customer Is Always Right!

Rule 2 If the Customer Is Ever Wrong, Reread Rule 1.

Our commitment to our customers is so solid that I had it carved into a three-ton granite rock that stands at the store's entrance.

Recognizing that the customer is always right has been the cornerstone of our business. Our Norwalk store is in one of the most competitive food-retailing areas of the country. There are more than ninety-three other food stores within fifteen miles of ours, and they are all selling basically the same things we are. When a customer walks into our store, she doesn't say, "What can I do for Stew Leonard's today?" She says, "What can Stew Leonard's do for me?" And if we can't do anything for her, she's not coming back. I don't blame her. Why should she? So my problem is the same as yours. How do we get customers to come back, week after week?

It's tremendously important to think like the person across from you—in our case, the customer. When I was in junior high school, my brother Leo taught me to play chess. I rarely won, and finally one day, I said to him, "Why don't I ever win?" He said, "Your problem, Stew, is that you are so interested in what you are trying to do that you don't give any thought to what I'm trying to do. Before I make my move, I mentally go around to your side of the table and look at the game from your point of view. Very often, after seeing things from your side, I improve my move." Running a business is a lot like playing a game of chess.

Looking at things from the customer's point of view helps to ensure that she'll come back each week. The average customer spends about $100 every week, and everything she has in her shopping cart will be eaten by her family during that week. So each week she makes a new buying decision: "Do

Most of our best ideas still come from our customers.

I go back to Stew Leonard's or do I go to one of those other ninety-three food stores?" If she comes back to us each week, she'll spend $5,200 in a year. And over ten years, she'll spend more than $52,000. So when we look at our customer, we don't see the lady with $100 worth of groceries in her cart; we see the $52,000 that she might spend with us over the next ten years and the profit that she'll bring to our business. That profit is our reward for listening to our customers.

The customer who complains is your best friend. She gives you the opportunity to fix the problem. It's the customer who doesn't complain who worries me, because she won't come back again. Statistics show that it costs five times more to get a new customer than it does to keep one you already have. So, at eight every morning, our suggestion box is unlocked and emptied. All the notes are typed up verbatim into a report, and the report is on every manager's desk by

11:00 a.m. Copies are even put on the tables in our cafeteria for all of our Team Members to read. Then we take action on them, the same day, not in four to six weeks, even though we receive more than 100 suggestions every single day.

The key to getting customer input is to take action. The first thing a shopper will do after making a suggestion is to visit the store again and see if you listened. If you did, she'll realize that you care, and very often she'll write more suggestions.

But we don't just wait for our customers to make suggestions. Each month we select fifteen to twenty customers at random and ask them for ideas to help us improve our store. We give them a $25 gift certificate for coming to an hour-long meeting. Most of them say they would come even if we didn't pay them for their time. They feel that our store is their store.

We start each meeting by saying, "What don't you like about our store? How can we improve?" We want to know what is important to them, what we can do better.

One customer told us that she didn't like buying fish in prepackaged Styrofoam trays with plastic wrapping. She said she preferred to see it on ice, the way it is displayed in fish markets. The very next day, we built a fish bar with our fish displayed right on the ice as she had suggested. We also continued to put out prepackaged fish in our refrigerated display cases. We discovered that some of our customers preferred to buy their fish from the counter, while others still liked to buy it already wrapped. And to our surprise, our fish sales doubled!

Another customer said she didn't like to buy strawberries in the little baskets with the big ones on top and the little ones on the bottom. She suggested that we put out the whole big tray, just the way the strawberries came from the farm.

"Why not allow customers to select and bag their own berries and pay by the pound?" she said. It sounded like a good idea, but when I went to our produce manager and said, "Let's try it!" He said, "Stew, that's the dumbest idea I've ever heard in my life! Don't you realize that as soon as

After a customer suggested that we put out flats of strawberries so people could choose their own, we found that they often bought more than they realized.

you put strawberries out loose, the customers will start eating them all?" I said, "Remember, Butch, the customer's always right." So we tried it. And the customer *was* right—our sales increased.

A couple of weeks later, Butch came running up to me and said, "Stew, I told you this was going to happen. Come quick!" He led me to the strawberry display where this big guy was lunching on our strawberries. I went over to him and gently said, "Sir, beautiful strawberries, aren't they? We'd appreciate it if you'd just sample one or two." He looked at me and said in a booming voice, "Go read your rock at the front door!"

Secret 2. Teamwork Is the Thing You Need; You Must Work Together to Succeed

My dad used to say, "Take good care of your people, and your people will take good care of your customers." He was right. Happy people deliver great customer service. There are several basic strategies that we use to build a happy team. First is reward. In his classic book *The Greatest Management Principle in the World*, Michael LeBoeuf tells a fable about a fisherman who was out in his boat one day. He had a fishing pole in one hand and a bottle of whiskey in the other. Suddenly he heard a thump on the side of the boat. He looked down and saw a little snake with a frog in its mouth. The fisherman felt sorry for the frog, so he gently took it out of the snake's mouth and let it go. The snake looked disappointed, so the fellow poured a little of his whiskey in the snake's mouth, and it swam away. About five minutes later, there was another thump on the side of the boat. The fellow looked down to see the same snake, this time with two frogs in its mouth! LeBoeuf's point is that what gets rewarded gets repeated.

One of the first things I would always do when I returned from a trip was to walk through our store, looking for everything that had been done right while I was away, and I would pat people on the back. The smiles on everyone's faces told me that people do not work just for money, they also work for appreciation. As Ken Blanchard points out in *The One Minute Manager,* too many managers catch somebody doing something wrong and criticize them for it. The result is that people tend to not stick their necks out; they play it safe instead. If you want people to take more initiative and become better managers, you have to praise them when they deserve it. You can't run your business alone; you need a good team.

Part of team building comes by looking at each person's point of view. It's easy to say this, but harder to do it. This is why I took Dale Carnegie's course twice. Then I went back as a "graduate assistant" to help teach classes. I even enrolled my family and all our managers. As Dale Carnegie taught, a successful leader learns to think in terms of the other person's interest. The goal is to get people to do what you want to do because *they* want to do it. From Dale Carnegie, we developed our own "MBA" program: Management By Appreciation. Through programs that show our appreciation of our Team Members' contributions, Team Members learn to think not of what is in their own best interest, but of what is in the best interest of the customer and of the store.

One day cashier Nicole was riding the bus to work and noticed several of the passengers were customers also on their way to our store. She wondered whether the bus driver would be allowed to drive her bus right into our parking lot and let shoppers off at our front door. The bus driver said she'd have to check with her supervisor. She did, he said he'd be willing to give it a try, and now, every couple of hours, a bus lets off several shoppers right at our front entrance. That year Nicole was presented with our ABCD Award. ABCD stands for Above and Beyond the Call of Duty!

One of my favorite quotes is from Bennett Cerf, who said, "A pat on the back, only a few vertebrae above a kick in the pants, is miles ahead in results."

One year Stew Jr. and I, along with several of our managers, were attending the Food Marketing Institute trade show in Chicago. Someone asked us, "Who's running the store while you're here?" Our reply was, "The same people who run it when we're there!"

Building a good team requires training. We spend more than $1,000 on training each Team Member every year, and it's one of the best investments we make. Train your team to do things the way you do. Teach your people all you know, constantly share information with them, and empower them to do what they think is necessary. Allow them to make mistakes, and encourage them to learn. Once they've learned, you can delegate to them.

When you build a strong team, it allows you to promote from within, and that creates great loyalty, because the good jobs go to the people who have earned them. Over 80 percent of our management today started in entry-level positions. We proudly display their photographs and names and the jobs they've held on "Up the Ladder" plaques throughout our store where everyone, customers and Team Members alike, can see them every day. The aisles of our store are like a trophy room. We want to show our Team Members that we are proud of them.

Just as you should think like your customers, you must think like your employees. They need good benefits and career opportunities: a great health plan, help with college tuition, the tools to get ahead on the career ladder, chances to earn overtime and holiday pay, bonuses when the store has a good season or a great year, and appreciation parties and free lunches. We offer a benefit program that is up there with the best in the business.

Contrary to the philosophy of many major corporations, we find it helpful to encourage family members to work together in our business. We find that if the mother or father is good, the son or daughter usually will be, too. Plus, that person will have two supervisors: a boss *and* a parent. Amazingly, about 50 percent of our Team Members have a relative also working at our store. The Flewellyn family at one time had seven members working together, from grandfather to grandson. It's a wonderful way to build pride and teamwork. Even my own four children all decided to work in our business.

But let me make one thing very clear. Although we believe in nepotism, we don't believe in favoritism! When my son Tom was younger, he dropped out of college and came home to work in our grocery department. One day, his manager came to me and said, "Stew, I've got a problem. Tom's college buddies wanted him to go to Fort Lauderdale with them during spring break. He asked me for the time off, but I told him it was too near Easter and he couldn't go. He went anyway. What should I do?"

I said I'd take care of it. When Tom returned, I sat him down for a heart-to-heart talk. (He later told me that he secretly thought he might have been missed so much that he was getting a promotion and a raise.)

I said, "Look, Tom, being a boss and also a father in a family business is tough. I have to wear two hats. One is as the boss, who has to be fair and treat everyone in the business the same. The other one is as your father, who loves you and wants the best for you. Here, let me first put on the boss's hat. Your manager told you that you couldn't take the time off to go to Florida, but you disobeyed and you went anyway. So you're fired."

He looked at me in total disbelief. I felt terrible. So I quickly said, "Now let me put on the father's hat. I hear you just lost your job, son. What can I do to help?"

Things eventually worked out. Tom went back to college,

and ten years later, he became the president of our second store, in Danbury, Connecticut.

There's an old saying: "If you want to be remembered in a year, grow corn. If you want to be remembered in fifty years, grow trees. If you want to be remembered beyond your lifetime, grow people." Train and reward the members of your team and they will take care of your business and your customers. Perhaps Walt Disney said it best: "You can design and create and build the most wonderful place in the world, but it takes people to make the dream a reality."

Secret 3: Excellence Is Not a Sometime Thing, It's an All-the-Time Thing

My goal from day one was to sell "fresh-from-the-farm quality at down-on-the-farm prices." One of my favorite sayings is a spin on a quote by Vince Lombardi, the football coach, who said, "Winning is not a sometime thing, it's an all the time thing." We have found that if we constantly strive for excellence, not only is that what we get, but it also affects how our customers view us. When customers see fresh-cut flowers in our restrooms every day, they know that somebody cares about excellence—and that if there are fresh flowers and the restrooms are spotless, our dairy plant must be spotless, too. Perception is everything.

Another way we strive for excellence is to sell only fresh bakery goods every day, starting from scratch each morning. Of course, we need to have baked goods on the shelves for those last few customers who come in before closing, so every night we have some left over. When the question came up of what do we do with these leftovers, because of our commitment to excellence, we didn't want to cut the price in half and sell the "Day-Old" bakery items to our customers. Instead, we turned this into an opportunity: we decided to help the community, giving all of our leftover products to the Salvation Army, homeless shelters, and soup kitchens. Early every morning vans and station wagons line up at our door as we give away yesterday's bakery products.

Excellence is also a way of thinking. We have a sign in our produce area that says "If You Wouldn't Take It Home to Your Mother, Don't Put It Out for Our Customers." That is our attitude about everything we produce in our kitchens and our dairy, and sell in our store.

That is also why our stores stock only 2,000 different items and yet our sales are several times greater than that of the average grocery store. At first we limited the number of items we sold because of space. But then I read about the Pareto rule and realized that it applied to our business. An Italian economist named Pareto defined what many now call the 80/20 Rule: in the food business, 80 percent of your sales will come from just 20 percent of your items. So in order to maintain our freshness and excellence, we only sell that 20 percent.

Once you have our formula for excellence in place, you have to make sure it stays in action. The way we do that is to be there with our customers and our Team Members on the store floor. We limit meetings and trips that take us out of the store, we talk to our suppliers right on the floor during the day, and our managers are all encouraged to spend as much time with customers as possible. Tom Peters coined a term for it: MBWA—Management By Walking Around. And it's a principle that I've always found to be true. In fact, my father had a similar belief: "The farmer's shadow is the best fertilizer."

Secret 4. WOW! Is What Our Customers Say, and When They Do, They Make Our Day

WOW! is the fourth secret to success. When you fail to promote, something terrible happens: nothing! People often say WOW! when they see our parking lot packed with cars. But to get their attention before they get to our parking lot, we installed a huge Las Vegas–style sign on the road right in front of our store. It's thirty feet high and has a digital display just like the big jumbo screens in football stadiums. We use it to advertise our truckload sales and to create a sense of excitement. If you stay excited about your store and your products, your customers will be excited, too.

Another favorite WOW! is the live country-and-western band hired during holidays. Then there are the musical Farm Fresh Five animatronics on display over the frozen foods section that makes the kids stop and dance. Children love the singing and dancing Chiquita Banana and our Moo Cow in the milk department, that goes "Mooooo" when they press

Costumed characters that roam our store are one of the reasons our customers' children beg their parents to come back.

the button or pull the bell around the cow's neck. We even have a model train that runs on a track above the refrigerator cases and circles the entire store. The whistle blows and the kids say, WOW!

We create the WOW! feeling of being on a farm with our little farm. There are baby calves, lambs, and chickens. And there are costumed characters like Clover the Cow and Daphne the Duck that walk around the store. Our Hit the Target Wishing Well collects more than $500 each week, which we donate to local charities.

Customers are always wowed by the great prices on milk and other dairy products; local produce; freshly made breads, cookies, and pies; beef straight from our ranchers in Kansas; fish right from the New York and Boston seafood piers; and seasonal items, from pumpkins to Christmas trees to truck-load specials of soda, chips, and other items.

But perhaps our biggest WOW! is what we call "Show and Sell." When we first opened with the dairy processing plant right in the middle of the store, customers loved seeing their milk being bottled and rolling off the conveyor belt. We built a platform for little kids, because they wanted to walk right up to the windows around it and watch the milk being processed. We also found that if customers can taste a sample of your bread or cheese or your apple cider, they'll be more likely to want to take some home. And if all of this doesn't make the customer say WOW!, we also thank them as they are leaving by giving them a free ice cream cone if they have spent $100 or more.

Some of our customers make *us* say WOW! A favorite of ours named Colleen Blanchard came up to me one day and said, "Stew, look!" She showed me a picture of her holding our shopping bag in front of St. Basil's Cathedral in Moscow. I was so proud of it that I put it up on our store's bulletin board with a little note: "Colleen Blanchard takes her Stew Leonard's shopping bag to Russia!"

I'd forgotten all about it until a few weeks later when I walked by the bulletin board and saw there were more photos tacked to it. There were customers with Stew Leonard's bags at the Acropolis in Athens! One customer was on a

When customers send us photos holding their Stew Leonard's shopping bags at famous landmarks, we put them up on the bulletin board in our store. Photos come in from all around the world!

Our first customer to do this was Colleen Blanchard, who gave me this picture from her trip to Russia. Another customer sent us his version of the moon landing.

Famous friends and customers posed for photos with our bags, including Lee Iacocca, pictured with Stew Jr. and me.

camel in the desert, in front of a pyramid in Egypt, another was on a pink sand beach in Bermuda. There were pictures of people at a body-building contest with Stew Leonard's bags, and customers holding our shopping bags on their wedding day. We now have thousands of pictures from all over the world, and we display them proudly on our "Bags Around the World" wall. We even have pictures of Bob Hope and Lee Iacocca holding Stew Leonard's bags!

If you take the first letter of each of these four secrets to success, you get our code word for our secret to success. STEW—"Satisfy the Customer," "Teamwork Gets It Done," "Excellence Makes It Better," and "WOW! Makes It Fun." *The Guinness Book of World Records* once made us say WOW! by listing us as having "the greatest sales per unit area of any single food store in the world." As Walt Disney said, "Do what you do so well that people will want to see it again and bring their friends." That is the philosophy behind STEW.

I ended my talk that day, and the moderator, Woody Woodruff, asked if there were any questions. As people asked how to get customers back and how to compete against Walmart's low prices, I started to think of even more stories I could share, more advice I could give, and ways I could try to help even more. When Warden Luther asked if I would work with the Chamber of Commerce again, my answer was an eager "I'd be honored."

Putting STEW to Work

I returned to my cube filled with ideas on how Bradford's business owners could approach their problems. I was inspired by the questions people had asked. The humiliation of being at the camp and its dreary, depressing culture faded against the prospect of helping the Bradford merchants' group. It was as if someone had suddenly shined a light on my dark and dismal days.

I no longer spent my time just mopping the training center floor, setting the tables for lunch, washing the dishes, polishing the windows, and making the mile-long trek from the dorm to the training center—those were just the things I did while my mind was racing with ideas I wanted to share with the Bradford merchants. I knew I could fill many meetings with suggestions and stories that could help them.

The one thing that nagged at me was that listening to a speech wasn't enough. I knew plenty of people would politely listen and then go back to their stores or offices and keep making the same mistakes they'd always made. How could I get them to use what they'd learned, to put their ideas into action? Then it occurred to me: wouldn't it be great if Warden Luther would allow us to create our own Bradford "Skunk Camp"?

Skunk Camp was an intensive brainstorming session that Tom Peters orchestrated for his clients. Stew Jr. and I had attended our first Skunk Camp in 1984. We spent four days with a group of executives from companies all over the country, listening to their stories of challenges, successes and mistakes, and we came away with a lot of ideas for improving our business. Perhaps such a session would help the Bradford merchants find the solutions they were looking for. When I wrote to Luther and suggested it, he agreed to allow me to give it a try.

That next Wednesday, about a dozen people came to the training center. Glenn and I asked everyone to help move the tables around so they formed a square in the middle of the room, and I explained the concept of Skunk Camp. I asked people to present their problems, to ask questions, and to offer possible solutions.

Soon the stories came flying! There were problems with customer service, with customer loyalty, with the competition from Wal-mart. There were dwindling populations and changes in people's needs and habits. There were name-recognition issues, branding problems, merchandise display challenges, and unsold inventory. We discussed them all. We came up with suggestions and ideas, and people agreed to try out the ideas and come back the next week and tell the group about their results. The Bradford Merchants' Workshop was born.

For example, a man named Howard Nickel owned a paint store called Jensen Paint Company.

"Who is Jensen?" I asked. He said he'd bought the store from Jensen fifteen years ago and that was what it was called.

"Why do you still call it Jensen Paint Company?" I asked.

He said that customers all knew the name and they were used to it. We encouraged him to change the name of his store to Nickel Paint & Decorating, and we sketched out a new logo. Soon he was planning a grand reopening, and the week after that he came to the workshop bursting with excitement. Customers who saw the "Grand Reopening" sign came in to see what was going on. Howard had gotten people to think of repainting or refreshing their homes, and sales went up. Howard laughed at how just mixing things up a bit could change people's perceptions.

"Some people came in and said 'I'm glad you finally bought this store, Howard!'" he told us.

Another merchant, Lester Brauser, had an outfitting store that sold camping equipment, clothing, and sporting goods. His store was the place to go for hiking boots, since hiking in the nearby Allegheny National Forest was a popular attraction. But tourists and others looking for hiking boots would learn of Brauser's shop only by asking around. The discussion turned to his big display window, filled with fishing gear and camping equipment. It was suggested that maybe he could replace all of the fishing and camping gear with hiking boots to create a WOW! That way everyone would know that was the place to go for boots.

Lois Miller, who owned a gift shop called Horizons, was struggling with managing her inventory and keeping up with her vendors. Part of the problem was that she was doing everything the old-fashioned way, even writing her receipts out by hand. She didn't have a computer, and she didn't know where to start. She was encouraged to computerize her store, and with the group's help, she got a computer expert to help her. Soon she was set up and connected not only with her vendors but with her customers, too.

Over the weeks, people offered other ideas as well. Most of the suggestions were basic common sense: to put the discounted clearance rack at the back of the store so customers had to walk past all the current merchandise to get to the sale items; to get more impact from their displays; to get rid of merchandise that took up space but didn't sell well; to simplify and reword restaurant menus so that the most popular items appeared special. Each week, the business owners were eager to attend the meeting to report on their week and describe their successes to the class as well as to learn from one another.

Glenn and I certainly looked forward to our weekly meetings with the workshop members. They were the highlight of our week and gave us tremendous satisfaction. During many of the meetings we would be honored with Warden Luther joining us. He seemed impressed with the enthusiasm of the group and the progress that the merchants were making.

That first week, the attendance was about a dozen or so merchants Woody and Ray had convinced to come and give it a try. But word quickly got out that our workshops were inspiring places, full of ideas, and before we knew it, we were approaching fifty members. Soon, merchants from nearby towns were asking to come to join the meeting too! We were even able to host meetings for the merchants from the town of Kane. One of the most surprising invitations came from the University of Pittsburgh. I was asked to come to their Bradford campus and give a presentation to the business students.

I truly felt that I was fulfilling my sentence in the best way possible: by doing something constructive for others.

chapter four

WHEN YOU FAIL TO PROMOTE, A TERRIBLE THING HAPPENS: NOTHING!

As we were entering our third year of business in our new location, I relied on three things: the instincts I gained from working with my father; Leo's common sense advice; and what I had learned at Dale Carnegie. From the three of them, I was able to see things from others' points of view and give honest, sincere appreciation for jobs well done.

It dawned on me that my managers would also benefit from learning the Dale Carnegie methods. At the time, our small business was made up of the men who had been milk deliverymen and dairy plant operators at the original Clover Farms Dairy. When we were forced to move, rather than replace our milkmen with skilled grocery people, I encouraged my men to accept the challenge with me—and every one of them did. My policy was to promote from within and reward their loyalty. Eventually, as the store grew, all of them stepped up to the plate and began dealing with customers, managing people, and even negotiating with suppliers—a far cry from loading trucks and delivering milk. One by one, I encouraged them to take the Carnegie course and then watched as they became versed in the art and skill of human relations.

One of the most effective principles that Dale Carnegie's course taught us was that "People don't listen in words, they listen in pictures." The concept worked so well in communicating person to person, I figured it would work in communicating with customers, too.

My advertising adviser Joe Shaw first asked me to make a list of the things I wanted our customers to know about our business. That was easy, I said: the quality of our milk and cream, our low prices, as well as other items too, like butter, eggs, and orange juice. But Joe told me that my list was too long and that I should focus on just one single customer benefit: he suggested that we concentrate on freshness! He then convinced me that rather than advertising all the attributes of our dairy, we should concentrate on creating an image that customers would be drawn to and remember. Joe used rough sketches and storyboards so I could better visualize what each new idea would look like. Together we worked to create newspaper ads, signs on our delivery trucks, even the images on our half-gallon milk cartons, all emphasizing something that our big supermarket competitors didn't have:

Joe Shaw taught me how to communicate visually.

milk so fresh you bought it right at our dairy plant; you'd have to own a cow to get it any fresher!

Joe's marketing skills helped us gradually build our little dairy store into a brand. Everything that we did made the Stew Leonard's name synonymous with "Fresh from the Farm." We tried to "talk in pictures" in all of our advertising and promotions.

These visual messages then came to life inside the store when Joe suggested that displays be built on bales of hay or on wooden farm wagons with hand-carved signs. Joe even taught me wood carving, and I took great pleasure in carving our own wooden signs that helped us increase our rustic farm image. Instead of displaying our ears of sweet corn on a shiny, metal refrigerated case like the supermarkets did, we built a corncrib in the middle of the aisle, complete with a wood-shingled roof. Throughout the day, as our crew of stock boys dumped burlap bags of fresh-picked corn into the corncrib, customers would crowd around and marvel that the corn was still warm from the field.

Soon the design of our signs on the outside of our building, on the sides of our trucks, and the ones that hung over our displays all had the same look, as if they had been created on the farm by the farmer himself. But one of Joe's best ideas was that my own handwritten signature become our company's logo to keep our brand image consistent, he said. At a time when most of chain supermarket competitors had corporate names, like ShopRite or A&P, a personal name like Stew Leonard's helped set us apart from the competition. In short, Joe helped us to create a simple, "down on the farm," fun-filled brand image.

Learning from the Master

One day Joe presented me with a book, *The Disney Version* by Richard Schickel, which detailed the history of Walt Disney and how he created his movie studio and theme parks. I devoured it, discovering that some of the very same challenges that Disney had gone through were familiar, especially the cry of the naysayers.

Prior to Disney World's opening, his critics speculated that no one would travel to the hot, buggy swamps of central Florida to visit an amusement park. But Disney wasn't discouraged. He once said that whenever ten people told him that one of his ideas was no good and wouldn't work, he then moved ahead with it because he knew that he probably had a winner.

Shortly before he died, Cinderella's Castle was built, standing majestically in the middle of a swamp. It was Disney's way of showing the naysayers that his dream was going to become a reality. He had said, "Always build your castle first. Let it be your vision to others to motivate them." But Disney's dream was more than just building a castle, it was his goal to create a place so exciting that people would want to come back again and bring their friends that intrigued me most.

I visited Disney World with my architect and friend Dick Bergmann. We spent two days roaming the park and studying the Disney way of doing things, and we were even privileged to be invited by management for a behind-the-scenes tour of the operation, including the underground level that houses all of the support systems for the park. I was impressed by Disney's use of the term "Cast Member" to describe everyone from Mickey Mouse and Donald Duck to the employees sweeping up peanut shells, because every Cast Member was "on stage" and each was an important part of the image of the park. I was especially amazed by the way the singing, dancing audio-animatronics and the costumed characters added to the fun. The excitement of Disney World made me realize that we might try to create a similar feeling in our store. We already had our little farm in front of our store and cows' heads on our trucks. It would be expensive but we could add audio-animatronics and costumed characters to create more excitement.

As we walked around the park, I continued to see ways in which Disney's philosophies might be applied at Stew Leonard's. The happy faces of children, the entertainment, the excitement all around was exactly the atmosphere I dreamed of creating at our dairy store.

But Disney's ideas went much further. He said that you must "give details top billing." I could see Disney's demand for perfection in the flowerbeds that were always vibrant and pristine, in the perfectly maintained facades of Main Street USA, even in the buttons and bows on the princesses' dresses. No detail was overlooked.

Disney's "all for one and one for all" philosophy emphasized the importance of teamwork and empowerment. Disney encouraged his Cast Members to follow their dreams and develop their talents. As a result, they came up with ways to improve rides, create new experiences, and add to the entertainment value of the parks. And when they weren't busy thinking of how to make the park a better experience, they were trying to make the park a better place by keeping it clean and well maintained. To see Disney's philosophy in action inspired me to form strategies that would keep our Team Members happy so that they, in turn, would keep our customers happy.

I especially related to the emphasis that Disney put on training; he knew that a business must constantly train and retrain its people. But what he accomplished was more than just showing Cast Members how to perform their jobs. On their very first day of work at Disney World, cast members were taught the philosophy of the company. On the plane trip home, my head was overflowing with ideas about how we might use Disney's principles to improve our own business. I couldn't wait to put some of his phenomenal ideas to work.

A Tough Man, a Tender Chicken, and a Good Friend

By 1975, our sales were growing rapidly. Our strategy continued to focus on fresh items, and we had slowly begun to add items like local produce, a salad bar, and fresh oranges from Florida. I regularly went on idea-gathering trips to successful farmer's markets in Pennsylvania and it became obvious to me that selling fresh chickens was a natural next step for us. When we added chickens, sales continued to climb. But I was surprised when customers began to request that we carry a particular brand of chicken, Perdue.

Frank Perdue had become famous in the marketing world for taking a generic product, chicken, and, with the help of the brilliant advertising man Ed McCabe, creating a brand name and a distinct product. Perdue had higher standards for chicken than the U.S. government had. To personalize the high-quality image of his chicken, Frank appeared in his own advertising campaign, where the announcer said, "It takes a tough man to make a tender chicken." The ads became so famous that Frank became a celebrity in his own right.

In addition to doing his own TV commercials, Frank was his own sales manager, overseeing the company's entire sales force. One day out of the blue, my secretary, Ann Ainsworth, buzzed me to say that Frank Perdue was in our waiting room. Frank, as it turned out, had read about us in the grocery trade magazines and heard about our high volume of sales, and being the ultimate salesman, he decided to stop at our store and see for himself. Frank used to visit New York City regularly to work with his advertising agency and see to other business obligations, and on one of his trips, he drove up to Norwalk to visit us.

Frank was warm and gracious and fascinating to listen to. He also seemed very interested in our business. I gave him a tour of the store, and then we went back upstairs to my office to talk.

I admired Frank Perdue because his standards were exacting.

"I'm amazed," he said. "I find it hard to believe that one store can sell as much chicken as you do! Why, some entire supermarket chains don't sell that much."

"Frank, I would consider giving you 100 percent of our business," I said, "if you could be a little more flexible on the price. Your chicken is more expensive than what I am buying now." I could see Frank calculating in his head as I talked; he was a shrewd negotiator, and I hoped he didn't want to walk away without a deal. After a little sparring we finally settled on a price, but Frank added one unusual condition: he insisted on seeing the large refrigerator where we store our milk and also would store his chicken. He personally wanted to check the temperature of the room.

I took him down to our big walk-in refrigerator. It was stacked high with cases of our fresh pasteurized milk. Frank took a little thermometer from his breast pocket and measured the temperature of the refrigerator.

"This will never do," he said. "I can't supply you with my chickens if you're going to store them in here. Thirty-six degrees might be okay for milk, but it's not cold enough for my chickens. If you want to store my chickens in here, you'll have to drop the temperature down to 33 degrees and maintain it there twenty-four hours a day."

I couldn't believe my ears. I'd never had a supplier tell me what temperature my cooler should be. Seeing my surprise, Frank said, "Look, Stew, either you drop the temperature in here to 33 degrees, or it's no deal. My fresh chickens require a lower temperature than fresh milk, period."

"Wow!" I thought, I guess he really is the "tough man who makes a tender chicken!" But then I also realized that Frank was a real quality fanatic, and I admired him for that.

From that moment on, Frank Perdue and I were friends. When Frank was in New York, Marianne and I would often drive into the city to have dinner with him. We soon discovered that we shared a mutual love for the Caribbean island of St. Martin, and we often vacationed there together. I was honored to have Frank as a friend; he inspired me. He was accomplishing things that I'd only dreamed about.

A few years after we began selling Perdue chickens, Frank announced that we were selling more of his chickens than any other single store. Soon a big ad appeared certifying that "Stew Leonard's sells more Perdue chickens than any other store in the world!"

Who Knew Butch Cassidy Was a Gourmet Cook?

One day my friend Bob Sharp called and asked if I would like to come with him to watch Paul Newman test his new race car in Lime Rock, Connecticut. Paul, who lived nearby in Westport, drove for Bob's Datsun team. Bob asked me to bring my video camera so I could record the tests they were going to perform on their new turbine-powered jet engine racecar.

The next morning, Bob and I picked up Paul at his house and the three of us headed up to Lime Rock. Over lunch, Paul asked how my store was going. I told him how sales were growing and how much I loved being in the food business.

Paul surprised me by saying "Stew, I'm trying to get into the food business myself." He went on to say that for years he and his friend A.E. Hotchner had been making Paul's salad dressing in his barn. He said that they enjoyed giving it to neighbors and friends as Christmas gifts. What made it so good was that they used only fresh all-natural ingredients and mixed and bottled it themselves in old wine bottles. "The dressing has become so popular that the neighbors keep clamoring for more," Paul said proudly. "I bet it would sell well in stores, too." I asked him why he would want to be bothered selling salad dressing to stores.

"It would be fun to become the Salad Dressing King of New England," Paul said, smiling his million-dollar smile. He explained that he and Hotchner were actually in the process of trying to do just that, but they had run into a wall trying to find a company that would bottle their salad dressing for them commercially. Paul wondered if I could bottle it for them at my dairy. I explained that it would be impossible because of the strict sanitation laws for milk and dairy products.

"But if you bring samples of your salad dressing to my office, I'll provide the lettuce and tomatoes, and we can make some salads and compare your dressing with some of the others that are on the market. If your dressing is as good as you say it is, I can help you find someone to bottle it for you." Paul loved the idea, so the next day I had Ann Ainsworth go out and buy about a dozen of the most popular brands at the local Grand Union.

A week later Paul, Hotchner, and Bob came to my office and we turned my desk into a salad bar. We poured Paul's dressing over bowls of lettuce and tomatoes and we all started sampling. Paul's dressing won hands down. The fresh garlic and herbs, extra virgin olive oil, and tangy vinegar were excellent together.

"You've got a great product there, Paul. I'll call Andy Crowley, who produces and bottles Ken's salad dressings for us, and I'll set up a meeting," I offered.

But Paul seemed less than enthusiastic. He said he'd already contacted Andy, who wasn't interested in bottling what he referred to as another "celebrity label" salad dressing. In fact, Andy had told Paul and Hotchner that he didn't even have time to meet with them.

What Paul didn't know was that Stew Leonard's was one of Ken's dressings' largest customers and that Andy and I were good friends. I also thought that Andy might be excited by Paul's path to the salad dressing business, since the Crowleys had a similar story: the salad dressing they served in their family-run restaurant was so popular that they began bottling it and selling it to grocery stores. I was certain that I would at least be able to persuade Andy to come to a meeting.

Sure enough, a couple of weeks later, Andy drove down from Boston to meet with Paul, Hotchner, Bob, and me

When Paul Newman asked for help starting his salad dressing business, we turned my desk into a salad bar and compared his dressing against the competition. His won, hands down. Bob Sharp, me, and Paul Newman.

in my office. I asked Paul to mix up some of his dressing right there for Andy to taste. We all sat munching on salad and discussing marketing Paul's dressing. Andy stressed the point that just because Paul Newman's name would be on the bottle, it would not automatically be a hit. He told us that many other celebrities had tried to market their own food products and they had not exactly set the world on fire with them: Frank Sinatra's pasta sauce, for example, Roger Staubach's peanut butter, Rocky Graziano's spaghetti sauce. Andy said that all of these products had "celebrity" on the outside of the bottle, but the product inside didn't make the customer want to buy a second bottle.

"But Paul's salad dressing is so good, I think that customers will buy the second bottle," I said. "In fact, Paul, with your picture on the bottle, it'll fly off the shelves," I continued.

"My face on a bottle of salad dressing?" Paul said. "Are you out of your mind? No way! And that's final!""

The conversation turned to some of the other hurdles. Paul wanted to bottle his dressing in wine bottles, just as he and Hotchner had always done, but Andy was insistent on using the same bottle that all of his other dressings came in. His bottling equipment could not be converted to handle wine bottles, he said. We also debated the properties and price of fresh versus freeze-dried ingredients. Again, Paul was in no mood to compromise.

"We have to use fresh, all-natural ingredients and extra virgin olive oil or the product just won't taste the same," he said.

Andy agreed to produce a first run of 1,000 cases, and he asked Paul for his home address so he could ship them to him. This stopped Paul in his tracks. "One thousand cases? I only have room in my garage for my Volkswagen!" For a minute, it looked as though the entire afternoon was sunk, but then I had an idea.

"I'll tell you what, Paul. I'll buy the first 1,000 cases," I said, "providing you agree to put your picture on the label!"

Stew Leonard's introduced Paul Newman's salad dressing to the world. Here, A. E. Hotchner, Paul Newman, and me at Paul's home in Westport, Connecticut.

Paul made a face and said he would have to think about it. He called me the next morning.

"Stew, I've changed my mind. I'll do it! I have a good friend, a fellow racecar driver named Sam Posey, whose wife is a terrific artist. She offered to do a drawing of me for the label." Sam's wife, Ellen, sketched Paul's picture, a line drawing that captured Paul's warm eyes and charming smile.

Not long after that, Newman's Own Salad Dressing became a reality. We introduced it to the world in my store, where we had most of the shipment of 1,000 cases piled high and big signs that read "Buy Two Bottles, Get a Free Head of Lettuce." We'd hung up one of the publicity photos that Paul had commissioned to promote the dressing. It was of Paul, Hotchner, and me dressed in Western wear. Paul was leaning casually on my shoulder, smiling his movie-star smile, and Hotchner was balancing a bottle of Newman's Own on my head. The caption under the photo read "Butch Cassidy Is Also a Gourmet Cook!"

Crowds of customers, along with lots of media and network television cameras from New York City, jammed the store all day long, and Paul's dressing was a hit. Within a few weeks, we had sold out of the first shipment and reordered, keeping Andy's production plant busy day and night. Some people were coming in and filling their carts with dressing—some for themselves and some to send to friends far away. In the first few months alone, we sold over 30,000 bottles. Even though Paul was only hoping to become the Salad Dressing King of New England, he was about to become the Salad Dressing King of the World!

Meeting Mr. Sam

One of the very early discount merchandisers was a company that got its start right near ours in Norwalk: Caldor. Founded by Carl Bennett and his wife, Dorothy, it grew from a few stores in Connecticut to one of the largest discount chains in the East. During the years that the Bennetts ran the company, Caldor was known for its high-quality products, low prices, and outstanding customer service, of which the Bennetts were especially proud.

I was an admirer of the stores and was fortunate enough to meet Carl one night at a Chamber of Commerce dinner. He invited Stew Jr. and me to come to lunch and see his operation. We met in his office, and then had lunch in his beautiful executive dining room. A sense of mutual admiration developed between us, and we became friends, getting together for dinner with our wives. Carl was also friendly with Sam Walton, the founder of Wal-mart. One day, Carl mentioned my name to Sam and told him he ought to visit my store. To Carl's surprise, Sam said he already had and was very familiar with it.

"Ask Stew if he would like to come to Little Rock to see the new Sam's Club I'm opening there," Sam offered. He said he would be at the grand opening of the store, one of the first of his wholesale clubs.

I was thrilled with the idea of meeting Sam Walton and seeing his new store, and I took Marianne and our four children with me. We flew to Arkansas the day before the grand opening. The store was still being stocked, and Sam—known as Mr. Sam to his associates in the company—met us there and gave us a tour. All of the store's 300 employees were busy putting out merchandise, setting up displays, cleaning, and getting ready for the next day. At the front of the store, a large stage had been set up, and after our tour, Sam climbed up on it and called all the employees to the front of the store and began one of his famous pep rallies. Sam was a natural cheerleader.

"It's great to see you," he said to the crowd, beaming with enthusiasm. "This store is going to be a huge success! You will be amazed!"

And then he began one of his famous team meeting cheers: "Gimme an S!" And the crowd cheered, "S!"

Then he yelled, "Gimme an A!" And the crowd shouted, "A!"

"Gimme an M!" And the crowed shouted, "M!" Sam led the crowd until they'd spelled out the name of the store.

"What does that spell?" The crowd hollered, "Sam's Club!"

Sam yelled, "Louder! I can't hear you!"

Pretty soon the whole place was exploding in thunderous cheers for "SAM'S CLUB! SAM'S CLUB! SAM'S CLUB!!!"

I was impressed with the tremendous enthusiasm Sam had generated. I also admired the layout of the store. There were ceiling-high racks filled with pallets of merchandise, everything from paper goods to TV sets and car tires, all at incredibly low prices. I could imagine how excited customers would be to shop there, and I could also imagine how successful Sam Walton was going to be.

Later that day, Sam asked if we would like to tour a few

After Sam Walton invited us to come to the opening of one of his new Sam's Club stores, we became good friends. He was never shy to ask for ideas.

of his other stores in the area. Soon we pulled up in front of a regular Wal-mart store. He took us inside and we walked around, Sam speaking with all of the sales personnel, calling them by name. At the end of our tour, Sam went over to one of the cash register booths, picked up a microphone that could be heard through out the entire store and began welcoming all of the customers to Wal-mart. You could tell that he really enjoyed talking to his customers. Then, just as we were leaving, Sam asked me if I had any ideas to make his store better.

"Well, I really can't think of anything I would improve. You have thousands of stores and I have only one. What could I possibly suggest to you?" I said.

But Sam insisted. "You must have seen something I can improve on," he said. I thought about it for a minute. "The only thing I noticed is that your associates' name tags all have their first two initials and their last name. It seems kind of formal. At Stew Leonard's, we only put the Team Members' first names to make it more personal and allow the customers to call the Team Member by his or her first name. We think it's a little warmer and friendlier."

Sam nodded his head in response, thinking over my suggestion. He then took a small tape recorder from his pocket and whispered into it.

A few weeks later, I received a letter from Sam thanking me for the suggestion and telling me that he had placed an order for 108,000 new name badges, one for each associate in his entire organization. Each one had only the employee's first name on it. I was so excited that I told Marianne about the letter from Sam as soon as I got home that night.

"Maybe before you made the suggestion, you should have gone into the name-tag manufacturing business," she joked.

Fortunately for Sam, he didn't listen to my other suggestion that day. After leaving Wal-mart, we followed Sam across town. He pulled into the parking lot of a large old supermarket. We went into the store with him and walked around.

"What do you think of this store?" Sam asked. It was a regular grocery store, nothing fancy or special. It didn't even seem busy, and the produce on the shelves didn't look fresh.

"I just purchased this store. We're thinking about going into the supermarket business," he said proudly. A grocery store operates very differently from the methods of a discount store or wholesale club store. I was sure it was the wrong direction for Sam's company to go in.

"I don't know, Sam," I said. "I think you might be making a big mistake. Selling butter and eggs is a lot different than selling TV sets. Freshness and turnover are the keys. I'd stick to the hard goods business if I were you."

Was I ever wrong! It was a good thing that Sam didn't listen to me. What I realized later was that it wasn't Sam's formulas for Wal-mart that would make his grocery retailing a successful venture, it was his underlying marketing philosophy—and with his brilliant management skills, he was able to make any business work.

A $28,000 Mistake and Worth Every Penny

On one of Frank Perdue's visits to Norwalk, he brought me his own personal copy of a book he had just finished reading.

"Stew, I think you'll like this." Frank handed me one of the greatest books anyone has ever given me: *In Search of Excellence* by Tom Peters and Robert Waterman. I took the book home that night and began to read it. I was mesmerized by it and couldn't put it down. I loved the stories of successful companies such as IBM, Xerox, and NCR (the company from which we had recently bought new electronic cash registers, becoming one of the first supermarkets to convert to 100 percent scanning with UPC codes). The book was filled with examples of companies that had built their businesses on the foundation of striving for excellence.

Many of the concepts I was trying so hard to build into Stew Leonard's were explained in detail in this book. Things like the importance of enthusiasm, really listening to your customer, and quality as a central ingredient to success. The book also helped me to see that our "Unique Selling Proposition," from a theory of marketing created by the advertising executive Rosser Reeves and made famous in his book *Reality in Advertising*, was firmly centered in our commitment to freshness, value, and customer service. Our "USP," as it was called, was what made us stand out from our competitors. I learned what a mission statement was, and the importance of "MBWA." It was the first time I had ever heard some of the terms, but not the first time I'd had similar thoughts. Peters and Waterman put into words what I believed and was practicing.

Peters and Waterman had discovered that successful companies viewed their employees as an asset rather than as an expense. They celebrated hands-on management, and praised companies that empowered their employees and recognized their efforts through special events from the annual holiday party to appreciation dinners.

I hoped that the company I was trying to build might become like those companies that Peters and Waterman raved about in their book. I went to bed that night thinking about creating a mission statement and what I would put in it, considering every value and philosophy that we used in our growing business. I woke up in the middle of the night and jotted down seven little words on a notepad I kept on the nightstand: "Our Mission Is to Create Happy Customers." I believed that as long as we could accomplish that, everything else would take care of itself.

I reread *In Search of Excellence* and discovered even more nuggets of wisdom. The more I read, the more enthusiastic I became. I bought copies of the book for Stew Jr. and Tom and then decided to give copies to all my managers as well. Reading *The New York Times*, I discovered that Tom Peters held *In Search of Excellence* seminars. I called Tom's office in California and found that he would soon be conducting a seminar at the Sheraton in Manhattan. I immediately purchased tickets for Stew Jr., Tom, several of our managers, and myself.

The meeting was held in one of the huge ballrooms at the hotel, a grand space with chairs for around 1,000 people. When we arrived, we went right up to the front and took seats in the first row. Soon Peters took the stage and began his speech. I was fascinated with his presentation. It was the first time I had ever seen someone speak using a slide projector with a giant screen. Rather than showing slides of diagrams, he showed big pictures of people! "People don't listen in words, they listen in pictures," I remembered.

Peters himself also fascinated me. He radiated tremendous enthusiasm and charisma. Every term, every phrase was a nugget of brilliance, and I tried to take it all in, to remember it so I could try to use it in my business. I took extensive notes; I didn't want to miss a thing. During a break, while people milled around the ballroom, I stayed in my seat, studying my notes. Suddenly Peters walked up to me and greeted me.

"I'm curious," he said. "I've never seen anyone taking so many notes. What are you writing?"

"Everything!" I replied. I explained how my friend Frank Perdue had given me his copy of *In Search of Excellence* and how much it had helped me. Then Tom and Stew Jr. told him about our store. He said he was familiar with it and had even stopped for a visit once on his way up to Boston. I was thrilled and asked if he would come up and talk to our entire organization.

"Sure," he said. "Just call my office and schedule the date." Later that week I called his assistant. She said he was solidly booked for months in advance and the earliest date open was in February of the following year. I booked the date.

Before I knew it, it was January and his secretary called to confirm the date I had reserved. I'd already alerted all our managers to be in the store that day because Tom Peters would be speaking in our conference room. But his secretary quickly dispelled that idea by explaining that he usually spoke in an auditorium. She also said that he always received his speaking fee paid in advance. I said that was no problem, expecting to have to send a check for several hundred dollars. Although it would be a lot of money for a small company like mine, I was sure it would be worth it. But her next words were, "Tom Peters's speaking fee is $28,000. Do you want to pay by check or with a bank transfer?"

I was completely shocked but didn't want to make a fool of myself by saying I couldn't afford it and canceling the date. I told her I'd mail a check and hung up the phone.

What was I going to do? I knew that having Peters speak to our managers would be of tremendous value, but I couldn't see how I could justify $28,000. His fee divided by my thirty managers came out to almost $1,000 each!

I had to come up with a way to turn this lemon of a problem into lemonade. And then a solution hit me. I'd book the largest meeting hall I could find, the ballroom at Long Shore Country Club in Westport, and I'd invite every influential person in town to be my guest! I had tickets printed up that read "*In Search of Excellence* author Tom Peters, Long Shore Country Club, ticket price: $1,000." For a month, I gave out free tickets to every town mover or shaker I could think of: city council members, the fire chief, the police chief, the mayor, my doctor and dentist, our suppliers, the board members of my bank, and practically every businessperson in the area. With a free ticket with a value of $1,000, everyone said they wouldn't miss it for the world. The truth was that every ticket was actually worth far more than $1,000.

Finally, February 16 came, and the ballroom at the country club was packed: standing room only! Peters gave a rousing speech that ended with a standing ovation that seemed to last forever. My managers were excited about our mission and our future, exhilarated by what they had learned that day, and overflowing with new ideas. And so was everyone I had invited. My guests were all impressed by the opportunity to learn from this best-selling author and inspired by what he said.

For months afterward, people came into the store to thank me for their ticket. Many had not heard of Peters before his talk, but he was quickly becoming nationally famous, featured on television news programs and in newspaper and magazine articles. *In Search of Excellence* went on to become one of the best selling business books of all times. Best of all, I felt lucky to have been the one to bring Tom Peters and his message to all of our town's leaders and businesspeople. My mistake had helped our town become a better place for everyone.

chapter five

+

STEW WHO?

The day I met Tom Peters at that first seminar, I was surprised that he had heard of us.

It was 1983, and our store had been growing steadily and was attracting customers from New York City as well as from other parts of New England. I had been in business for fourteen years. But although the food industry trade papers and the local media wrote an occasional story about our uniqueness, we had not received any national media attention.

My friend and Westport public relations expert Leo Miller had helped me promote Clover Farms Dairy locally during my early milk delivery days. Now I called on him again, but he told me that he had retired. However, he recommended his former top assistant, a clever woman named

B. L. Ochman, who had moved to New York City and opened up her own agency.

B. L. was a real dynamo and an experienced professional. She quickly got to work garnering the attention of some New York City publications. Then one day, out of the blue, we received a call from a *New York Times* reporter named Bryan Miller. Bryan happened to live in Westport and was familiar with our store. It was an extremely busy Saturday when he arrived to interview me. Our parking lot was packed, and many of the cars had New York license plates, which meant most had driven many miles and passed many other food stores to shop with us. Bryan seemed especially interested in the reasons there were so many customers flocking from so far away. I attempted to answer his question with a little rhyme that I often used to sum up our marketing philosophy: "We lower the price and sell the best, then let word of mouth do the rest."

Being a food expert himself, Bryan liked our focus on freshness and quality. He noted that we either produced our own products, like our milk and bakery items, or bought directly from the source, cutting out the middlemen. We toured all of our departments and I showed him behind the scenes (our milk production dairy, ice cream plant, and large warehouse brimming over with name-brand, nationally advertised products.). He also seemed to get a kick out of our little farm and all of our WOW!s as well. Along the way, Bryan stopped and asked questions of Team Members and customers. He seemed to have a good time, but when he left, I wasn't sure what type of impression it all had made on him.

A few days later, B. L. Ochman called me. She was very excited.

"I've got some great news for you, Stew. I just received word that your store is going to be one of the feature stories in tomorrow's *New York Times*."

Marianne and I couldn't believe our eyes when we opened the paper early the next morning! Emblazoned across the top of the front page of the Living Section was the headline "In Norwalk, a 'Disneyland' Dairy Store," along with a big picture. All I could say was WOW! Bryan referred to me as "a walking font of aphorisms." At first, I didn't understand what he meant, until Marianne explained that it was due to all of the quotations I often use when describing my business. In explaining the importance of advertising and the excitement we had created around our specials and in-store promotions, I quoted Stewart Britt, the great advertising genius, who said, "Doing business without advertising is like winking at a girl in the dark. You know what you are doing but nobody else does." To explain why I focused so closely on every little detail of the business, I repeated one of my favorite sayings: "Winners focus and losers spray."

The story even included some of our sales figures: "Mr. Leonard sells 10 million quarts of milk a year, not to mention a million pints of cream, a million cartons of yogurt, 100 tons of cottage cheese, a million dozen eggs, and equally staggering quantities of 600 other products." The story went

"All the News That's Fit to Print"

The New York Times

Late Edition

VOL. CXXXII . . . No. 45,717 — NEW YORK, WEDNESDAY, JUNE 22, 1983

In Norwalk, a 'Disneyland' Dairy Store

By BRYAN MILLER

NORWALK, Conn.

"MY dream ever since I was a little boy was to be a milkman," Stew Leonard recalls, leaning back in a chair in his office here. "My family was in the dairy business — that's what I knew best and it's all I wanted." To say that Mr. Leonard has realized his dream is somewhat like saying the astronaut Neil Armstrong made good on a boyhood fantasy of flying an airplane.

Mr. Leonard sells 10 million quarts of milk a year, not to mention a million pints of cream, a million cartons of yogurt, 100 tons of cottage cheese, a million dozen eggs and equally staggering quantities of 600 other products. He has not driven a delivery truck since the late 1960's, when the state of Connecticut furrowed a highway through his dairy farm. But Mr. Leonard says he remains essentially a milkman — perhaps the most successful one in America.

Stew Leonard's, which bills itself as "The World's Largest Dairy Store," is a most remarkable success story in American food retailing. More than

The New York Times sent a reporter to write about our store, and when we saw this headline we couldn't believe our eyes.

on to say, "More than 100,000 customers enter his sprawling, aseptically clean milk plant-grocery store annually. To say that Mr. Leonard has realized his dream is somewhat like saying the astronaut Neil Armstrong made good on a boyhood fantasy of flying an airplane."

But what really thrilled me was that the article gave credit to Walt Disney for what I had learned from him: "Mr. Leonard's role model is Walt Disney, whom he calls 'the the most creative marketing genius ever,' and Disney's influence is evident throughout the store."

A Maniac with a Mission

The story created quite a stir and soon attracted interest from other publications, including the *International Herald Tribune* and *INC, People,* and *Fortune* magazines. We soon were amazed to be featured on the television programs *PM Magazine, 20/20,* the CBS Evening News, ABC World News, and CNN.

As thrilled as we were that B. L. was able to generate so much media attention, what was about to happen next made me jump with joy. Tom Peters called to ask if he could send a film crew to our store. He was producing an *In Search of Excellence* series for PBS and wanted to include Stew Leonard's in it. To say that I was honored would be the understatement of the century.

A week or so later, John Nathan of John Nathan Productions met us as our store with a camera crew. They spent the day talking to Stew Jr., Tom, and me, asking us to explain our management philosophy and getting us to tell stories about our business and our customers. As we walked the store, the producers paused by the suggestion box and asked me why ours was oversized and so prominently displayed.

"It's one of the most valuable things we have in our entire store," I explained. When I first opened, I installed it because, as a milkman, I wasn't familiar with running a retail food store, and I decided to ask the advice of the people who were: My customers! When we first put it up, several people told me that they bet that most people wouldn't go to the trouble to write me a note.

"Everybody knows that no business ever actually reads suggestion notes from customers," they said. But I decided that at Stew Leonard's, I would do things very differently. Every morning at 8 a.m., I took great pride in unlocking the suggestion box myself and learning exactly what my customers were thinking. Some days the notes were so interesting that I stood right there in the middle of the store until I had read every single one.

My interest didn't go unnoticed by my customers. They could see that I truly cared about what they were writing me. Sometimes I would even call a customer who had written a note to discuss it further. I figured that if they cared enough to take the time to write notes to me, I should care enough to make the time to respond.

All of this listening soon began to really pay off. Most of the notes were complaining about something wrong, which I immediately fixed. Some were even compliments. And some were ideas that might seem off the wall but turned out to be the very best notes of all. A few were brilliant and worth their weight in gold. For example, one said, "You leave your shopping carts outside and on rainy days they get all wet. When I put my twin daughters in the shopping cart seat, they get all wet, too. You ought to do something about that!" The customer's note made a lot of sense to me, so before the next rainy day, we built a paper towel stand near the door with a big sign that read "Help Yourself to Paper

Towels to Dry off Your Shopping Cart!" We started doing what our customers suggested, and we found that the more we listened, the more good suggestions we got.

"Some of the ideas are so valuable," I told the producer, "I can't for the life of me understand why every store in America doesn't have a large customer suggestion box. But the bottom line is that the owner of the company *must* care enough to read each day's notes." I was so passionate talking about all the little details of our business, right down to the suggestion box, that I completely forgot about the lights and TV camera.

A few months later, Marianne, our daughters Beth and Jill, and I gathered in our den with Stew and Tom and their wives to watch the debut of *In Search of Excellence*. We sat breathlessly as the narrator told stories of IBM and Disney, with behind-the-scenes views and interviews with their executives. Then, in a flash, just after the story on Disneyland, came a shot of our store, just inside the entrance. The story started off with a customer's WOW! reaction at seeing our store for the first time. She said, "I've never seen anything like it before in my life!"

"This isn't Disneyland," the narrator said, and he began to describe our store. We laughed with excitement, thrilled to see our little dairy store on national TV! Soon the screen was filled with shots of customers and costumed characters and musical animatronics. It showed the fun and excitement of happy customers, everyone smiling and laughing.

I was laughing, too, as the host said, "Stew Leonard is

a maniac with a mission" as the cameraman followed me through the bakery department. He then went on to tell how we had started as a dairy and were now buying beef directly from ranchers in Kansas and fresh produce from farms in California.

"Stew Leonard's sells only 750 items, yet has sales of $1.5 million a week, four times that of an average supermarket," he continued.

Then they focused on our suggestion box. One of the secrets to our success, the narrator said, was that we listened to our customer and reacted. Our strawberry displays? Customer suggestion. The pack-your-own-eggs station? Customer suggestion. The fresh fish counter? Customer suggestion. Almost every story the show focused on was one in which we had listened to our customers and put their good ideas to work.

The next day, friends called with congratulations. People stopped me in the store to say how thrilled they were to see "their store" on TV. Even suppliers from as far away as Florida and Chicago called to say they had watched the show.

Then a surprising trend began. As word spread, company executives from around the country began having their secretaries call to see if they could arrange a tour of our store. Of course we were happy to oblige, and soon some of our management was spending quite a large portion of time conducting tours. But just as Sam Walton had done with me, we were sure to ask each visitor, "Can you suggest just one idea that we might use to make our store better?" Usually we received more than one and would quickly try them out.

Inside Tom Peters's Skunk Camp

That spring, Frank Perdue stopped by to see me with an invitation: would I like to go with him to Tom Peters's "Skunk Camp," an intense five-day informal seminar? Top executives from all over the country would be there. The seminar would focus on each company's management and marketing practices, and by attending, we could learn how these companies had achieved the success they had. We would be invited to tell our own stories to the group as well, and everyone would share their problems and ideas. Frank was sure that we would come away with a lot of ideas and information that we could put to good use. Did I want to go? WOW! I wouldn't miss it! I immediately called and made a reservation for Stew Jr. and myself, and a month later we were on a plane with Frank and his son Jim, on our way to California for our first "Skunk Camp."

The camp was held at a resort tucked into the coastal California hillside just south of Monterey, called Pajaro Dunes. We checked into our hotel, and then headed to the seminar registration desk. There we met two of Tom's associates, Jayne Pearle and Nancy Austin, who were handing out the materials we would need. In front of them, spread out on the table, were the name tags of some of the people we would become friends with. There were several names I recognized: Tom Malone, president of Milliken & Co.; Donald Burr, founder of the no-frills airline People Express; Tom Monaghan, founder of Domino's Pizza; Hal Rosenbluth of travel services company Rosenbluth International; John Fisher, the technology expert from Bank One of Columbus, Ohio; John McConnell of the steel company Worthington Industries; Bob Buckman of the chemical company Buckman Labs in Memphis, Tennessee; and Bill Gore of W. L. Gore. Stew and I were excited to be in the same room with these business icons and thrilled to be a part of a seminar with such brilliant minds.

For the next few days, we met in a group, listening to Peters and his guest speakers, asking questions, offering ideas, and telling stories. We went from being strangers to being friends, and from not knowing much about each other's companies to having an intimate knowledge of their problems and strategies. And I soon discovered one thing we all had in common: each person was a "follow-through" type. When a good idea came up, they acted on it. Even during breaks between sessions, the phone bank was busy with seminar attendees relaying ideas back to their companies to get their teams moving. That week, some set up new management training programs or new compensation plans. Others improved their quality control. Frank and Jim Perdue even started their own "Perdue University" after hearing about other corporate universities at the camp.

One afternoon, Tom invited a few of the class members to

give presentations and tell the group about their companies. Bill Gore, the genius inventor who created Gore-Tex, told one of the stories that fascinated me. He especially impressed Stew Jr. and me because of the empathy he had for the people who worked in his several factories.

He told us about Mabel, a hardworking woman in one of his factories. She had been on the assembly line for many years. One day she came to his office and said, "Mr. Gore, lots of people around here have business cards and I don't have one."

"Well, I'm sorry about that, Mabel. I'll see what I can do. What is your title?" Bill asked her.

"That's the problem, Mr. Gore. I don't have one," she said.

"Well, what title would you like?" Bill asked.

She said she had to think about it overnight.

"No problem," Bill said. The next morning, Mabel came back to his office and told him that she knew the title that she wanted on her business card. A few days later, Bill appeared at Mabel's station on the assembly line with a box of her own business cards. Prominently under her name was her new title: "Supreme Commander."

After Bill told the story, he explained how important he felt it was for all of us to respect and show empathy for our employees. He went on to say that from that day forward, he referred to all of his employees as associates instead of employees. He emphasized the importance of having each person feel that he or she is an important member of the organization.

Bill's story impressed Stew and me so much that we decided to take a page out of his book and stop referring to our people as employees. That night over dinner, we kicked around the idea of respect and titles. Bill's "associate" title didn't seem to fit our operation, and we realized that what made our store work so well was that we all felt we were members of a team. In fact, teamwork was the T in my "STEW" speech. We decided that from that moment on we would refer to all of our employees as Team Members, with a capital T and a capital M.

I didn't realize that during this incredible week, as Tom Peters led us through the ups and downs of excellence and marketing, he was also collecting material for his next book, carefully selecting the companies he would include. Not long after we returned home from Pajaro Dunes, he called to say that he was going to profile Stew Leonard's in his new book, *A Passion for Excellence.*

A Passion for Excellence and *In Search of Excellence* were not just best selling business books; they were responsible for creating a worldwide excellence movement in the entire business world. Companies of all sizes were eager to adapt the ideas that Peters wrote about. And executives across America wanted to learn even more than the books revealed, so they approached the people featured in the books and invited them to speak at their corporate meetings. I began getting more and more of these invitations, and felt it was a real privilege to be asked. In the several months after *A Passion for Excellence* became a best seller, Stew Jr. and I were

Best selling author Tom Peters wrote about us in his books on excellence, putting Stew Leonard's on the map.

invited to speak at meetings of Chase Manhattan Bank, Kawasaki, the Cleveland Creativity Symposium, Washington & Jefferson College, Citibank, Perdue Farms, and the Coca-Cola Company. The University of Michigan's Creativity Symposium even invited me to come and give the keynote address.

Scared Out of My Wits

The first talk I was ever invited to give in front of a large audience was in 1985, and it was a speech I'll never forget. One day, while I was busy talking to customers in the store, my friend Cal Walker, the Connecticut sponsor for Dale Carnegie, called.

"Stew, I was asked by headquarters to invite you to be the keynote speaker for the International Dale Carnegie Convention in Atlanta."

"Are you kidding me, Cal? I've never given a keynote speech in my entire life," I said.

"No problem," he said. "I'll be glad to help you prepare."

After all that the Dale Carnegie organization had done for me, I realized it would be great to thank them in person. Although I was tremendously honored, I was scared to death by Cal's invitation! As he promised, though, he coached me through my rough spots. He readied me for what I considered to be the pinnacle of public speaking, talking to an audience of hundreds of Dale Carnegie instructors from all over the world, as well as Dale Carnegie's widow, Dorothy Carnegie.

When the big day came and Cal introduced me, the audience politely applauded, and I made my way to the podium. I looked out at the group, took a breath, and began. Soon I looked up to see relaxed, smiling faces, and I was relieved. The audience was warm and wonderful. They laughed at my little jokes and seemed to enjoy the slides of our business that illustrated my key stories: the eggnog story, the story about the rock at our front door, and the cow heads on our delivery trucks that go "*mooooo.*" I even told them about our "Bags Around the World" bulletin board. Then, near the close of my speech, I surprised the audience by saying that I had placed a Stew Leonard's plastic shopping bag under each of their seats and I asked them if they would all hold one up so I could take a photograph of them from the stage. "My customers back in Connecticut will never believe this!" I said. They loved the idea and held up their bags with cheers and laughter, and then they gave me a standing ovation. Afterward, many people came up and amazed me by asking if I'd autograph their bags; I spent more than an hour signing them. Wow! What a group!

Later that day, I was able to meet with Dorothy Carnegie. She told me how she enjoyed the enthusiasm that I brought to the stage and the stories I told, and then, in one of the most touching moments of all, she said that she only wished Dale had been alive to hear me speak. Talking with her that day, and addressing the audience of Dale Carnegie instructors, was one of the great privileges of my life.

Preaching to the Choir

Soon after I returned from Atlanta, I received a call from Greg Anderson, the executive vice president of Crystal Cathedral Television Ministries in Garden Grove, California. Like so many millions of readers, Robert Schuller at the Crystal Cathedral was enthralled with the stories in Tom Peters's books. Greg had even called Peters and invited him to speak at one of their symposiums, a regular gathering of 500 entrepreneurs and businesspeople in the Orange County area. The meetings, which brought together top leadership speakers to share their business experiences and expertise, were held on the cathedral campus and the keynote address was delivered on the altar inside the incredible glass cathedral, a monumental structure twelve stories high and larger than a football field.

Despite the impressive size of the symposium audience, and the world renown of the Crystal Cathedral, thanks to the weekly television program *Hour of Power,* which regularly drew millions of viewers, Peters was not able to work their invitation into his busy schedule. For Greg and his group, it was back to the drawing board. But the answer came easily: They decided to invite several of the people who were featured in Peters's books. And luckily, I was one of them.

Our store was not familiar to people in California, and most of the other speakers represented companies that were much better known than mine, so I was honored to be invited. Later I found out that Danny Cox, who was the head of the selection committee and who has since became a great friend, said that the story of our small company and its philosophy appealed to the group.

To me, it was such a big deal to be asked to speak at the cathedral that I brought our whole family to California for the event: Marianne, Beth, my sister Dot, Stew Jr. and Kim, Tom and Karen. Jill and her soon-to-be-husband, Rocky, drove up from San Diego, where they were students at the University of San Diego, and Kim, who grew up in nearby San Marino, invited her parents, Paul and Barbara, and her brother Robert to attend, too.

I decided to talk about our business philosophy and

summed it up with the acronym STEW, for Satisfy the Customer, Teamwork Gets It Done, Excellence Makes It Better, and WOW! Makes It Fun!

After my presentation, Danny, who had been the master of ceremonies, asked if I would like to have breakfast the next morning with Dr. Schuller. I enthusiastically accepted. In the coming months, Danny invited me back to speak at their "Possibilities Thinkers" luncheon and again I was invited to dine with Dr. Schuller and his lovely wife, Arvella. Dr. Schuller then had yet another proposal for me.

"Stew, how would you like to be my guest on my *Hour of Power* TV broadcast? Your story will be inspirational to our audience." I couldn't believe my ears. I had heard that more than 100 million people viewed Dr. Schuller's weekly program worldwide, now that the broadcast had even begun to be carried in Russia! I didn't hesitate with my answer.

"Wow!—I'd be honored!" I said.

A few months later, Marianne and I flew back out to California. Dr. Schuller, dressed in his trademark light blue robes, gave me a kind introduction from the pulpit of the cathedral. Then, in his friendly, warm manner, he called me forward and asked me questions about how I had gotten started as a milkman and what I felt were the keys to business success. The next several minutes literally flew by and before I knew it, it was over. Speaking to the Crystal Cathedral congregation and to the millions of people in the worldwide TV audience was a thrill of a lifetime!

After the church services, Dr. Schuller told me about a

Prior to being a guest on Dr. Robert Schuller's Hour of Power *television program we chatted in his office.*

new book he had just written, *Tough Times Never Last, but Tough People Do.* He was planning a book-signing tour, and I invited him to do a book signing at my store. The following month, we arranged for him to come to our store and spend an afternoon with us. I placed advertisements and announcements in the newspapers, and our electronic road sign flashed, "Welcome Dr. Robert Schuller!" He landed nearby in a helicopter and was driven to a store packed with an unbelievable crowd. There wasn't a single empty space in our parking lot, and the lines to meet him were so long that they wound all the way through the store and out around the building. Customers could not even push their shopping carts through the aisles.

As we walked into the store together that day, the image of Dr. Schuller as an eminent pastor and celebrity faded away when he told me of the memories the sight of our silo brought to him. He was raised on a farm, he said, and his dad used to always say to him, "Robert, remember, you have a big responsibility. The cows have to be milked twice every day, come hell or high water!"

It was then I understood that Dr. Schuller could see life from the same perspective as everyone else, and that made his wisdom all the more special. It was no surprise that so many people came to buy a signed copy of Dr. Schuller's book that we ran out of copies!

My Disney World Education

Besides being a good friend, Danny Cox is a best-selling author and one of the country's finest motivational speakers. He is also a great admirer of Walt Disney, just as I am. Not long after our meetings at the Crystal Cathedral, he called me to say that he had heard that Disney was introducing a seminar at Disney World called the "Disney Approach to People Management," a three-day course held in Orlando. I had attended Disney's seminars in the past and found them to be motivating and educational, and this new one, focusing on team management, seemed especially interesting. Danny and I agreed to attend together.

Each day of the seminar we attended classes, and in the evening Danny and I would have dinner and discuss all of the ideas presented that day. Our meals became brainstorming sessions as we reviewed what we had learned.

During one of the classes, our Disney hosts gave us an after-closing tour of the Magic Kingdom. It was just as magical as it had been on my first visit behind the scenes. We were shown how everything comes together while guests are not in the park, how the Cast Members work around the clock to make Walt Disney's dream come true.

Because Stew Leonard's had been featured in Tom Peters's books and television show alongside Disney, our seminar leaders seemed especially cordial and happy to have us as guests in their park. I was even invited to meet with their executive management and speak at their board of directors meeting. The Disney executives rolled out the red carpet and taught us what southern hospitality was all about. As a final bonus, they even invited me to ride as Grand Marshal of the Disney parade the next afternoon.

All I could say was, WOW! The parade, which features all the Disney characters from Mickey Mouse to Cinderella, is one of the highlights of every guest's visit to Disney World. That day I got to ride up front with Cinderella on an antique "horseless carriage," next to Mickey Mouse, who was dancing in the street and waving at all the people lining the parade route through the park and down Main Street

After the seminar I was Grand Marshal of the famous Disney World parade down Main Street.

USA. I'm sure that those people didn't know who I was, but I did: I was the luckiest milkman in the world.

I think, as the prizefighter Rocky Graziano said, "Somebody up there must like me," because it seems that I've had incredible luck in finding a silver lining in most every cloud.

When the state of Connecticut condemned our Clover Farms Dairy property in order to construct their new Route 7 Highway, I was forced out of business. But at that time, milk delivery was becoming a thing of the past, and I was being presented with a golden opportunity to start over. At the time, I didn't know where I was going to get the capital I needed to build a new business. By luck, one day I ran into my friend Phil Baker. He owned a restaurant practically right next to the dairy, and he was being forced to relocate his restaurant, too. He told me that he had applied to the Small Business Administration and was given a low-interest loan to help him make his move. I had never even heard of the SBA, but he suggested that I should look into applying for an SBA loan myself.

I immediately called the SBA's office in Hartford. With the help of my friend and attorney Tom Flaherty, we began the long application process. Our goal was to borrow approximately $485,000. The process certainly wasn't easy and involved piles and piles of paperwork, but finally, with Tom's tremendous persistence and determination, we won the SBA's approval.

Soon the SBA people became my best friends. They offered me more than just loans. They had resources, publications, and advice for small entrepreneurs like me, and I took advantage of many of their offerings. As Stew Leonard's grew, they decided to use us as one of the success stories of the Connecticut SBA chapter. I was so grateful for all the SBA's help over the years that when George Solomon, who was an adviser to the federal government on business affairs, asked me to speak to the SBA World Conference for Small Business in 1986, I was eager for the opportunity to thank them in person. A few months later the agency

It was a great honor to receive the Presidential Award for Entrepreneurial Excellence from Ronald Reagan at the White House in 1986.

announced that they had named me the Connecticut chapter's "Small Business Advocate of the Year." Yes, the SBA is the small entrepreneur's friend, that's for sure. Without its help, there would be no Stew Leonard's.

One day, George Solomon called to say that he had nominated me for the Presidential Award for Entrepreneurial Excellence, which was being given in Washington, D.C. to a small group of entrepreneurs. Recipients would be invited to the White House where they would meet President Ronald Reagan, who would personally present the awards. The day following the ceremony, each of the recipients was scheduled to speak at a luncheon, and I would be part of a dais of entrepreneurs including my friend, Wally "Famous" Amos, who created the cookie company.

Marianne and I flew to Washington, and I received the award from President Reagan. Suddenly, after the ceremony, I began to feel dizzy and sweaty and had to go back to my hotel room and lie down. The stress of the business, the craziness of my schedule, and being at the White House—all the pressure had caught up with me.

The next day, I could hardly get out of bed to give my scheduled talk, and I was forced to bow out of the affair. Marianne changed our airline tickets so we could fly home immediately. During the flight back to New York, I passed out, and when I woke up, the plane had landed and there were flight attendants and emergency medical technicians all around me. I was rushed right to the hospital emergency room, where the doctors did test after test. Finally, after a few blood transfusions, it was determined that I'd passed out due to a loss of blood: I had bleeding ulcers.

Soon after I returned to Norwalk, I was back on my feet. The New York Sales Executive Club announced that they were honoring Tom Peters at their annual luncheon, and they invited me to introduce him. The luncheon was held in the New York Sheraton Center ballroom, and there would be more than 500 in the audience, including important corporate executives, some of the most successful salespeople in New York, and celebrities. After lunch it was time for me to introduce Tom Peters, and as I stood at the podium looking out at the audience, which included Barbara Walters, Tom Brokaw, and Malcolm Forbes, I announced that I wanted to introduce a special friend of his who had flown all the way from his famous Skunk Camp in California just to be here. And from behind the curtain appeared my son Tom, all dressed as a full-sized Disney-style black-and-white skunk character!

I introduced Tom Peters at the New York Sales Executive Club. We surprised Tom by having my son Tom dress up in a skunk costume and jump out from behind the curtain in honor of Tom's famous Skunk Camp.

We were all laughing so hard that I became a little flustered, and I asked the audience to please help me welcome Tom Peters, the author of the best seller *In Search of SEXCELLENCE.* Tom turned red and roared with laughter as we switched places at the podium.

A Trip to the Big Leagues

But by the early 1990s, it was time to slow the pace and hand over the public speaking to my sons, Stew Jr. and Tom.

That's when I received an offer, like in *The Godfather* movie, "that I couldn't refuse." Danny Cox invited me to be the keynote speaker at the Annual National Speakers Association convention in Palm Desert, California. The audience would consist of thousands of speakers from all over the world. After my early experience of speaking to the Dale Carnegie organization, I knew that I was in for a fun time. Professional speakers are the most wonderful audience you can ever imagine, and this one in particular was an enthusiastic group—even though I thought that my every word and twitch and gesture might be studied and analyzed. I consider being the keynote speaker at the National Speakers Association a dream come true.

It was also a tremendous honor to be included among such an elite group of people who had given the keynote speech in the past; one of those men was Dr. Norman Vincent Peale.

When we learned that Dr. Norman Vincent Peale and his wife were fans of our chocolate cookies, Tom and I made a special delivery.

Dr. Peale and his wife, Ruth, were good customers of our Danbury store. They lived in nearby Pawling, New York, and often drove over to Danbury to do their food shopping. One day they invited my son Tom and me to pay them a visit. We loaded our car with gifts and goodies such as chocolate chip cookies and fresh-roasted coffee beans, and we spent an enjoyable afternoon with them. Knowing that I had been the keynote speaker at the NSA convention the previous year, Dr. Peale told us how he had spoken to the group a couple of years before himself. He told us that as he was taking the hotel's elevator down to give his talk; a fellow wearing an NSA nametag stepped into the elevator. Dr. Peale asked him if he was going to hear the speaker. The guy said, "No, I hear some preacher is speaking. I bet it's going to be boring!"

In 1991, Sam Walton was inducted into the National Sales Hall of Fame, which was held at the Waldorf-Astoria hotel. I reserved a table at the awards dinner and took a group of eleven. It was an over-the-top black tie affair, and the room was filled with important people from the New York area. We were thrilled to celebrate Sam's honor with him. But the real honor, for me at least, was the next day. Sam invited Marianne and me, along with Carl and Dorothy Bennett, to an intimate luncheon to celebrate Sam's eightieth birthday. We had lunch at the Four Seasons, famous for its power-broker clientele, soaring ceilings, and sleek modern design. During lunch, we talked about all getting together again at our home in St. Martin.

A few days later, I received a letter from Sam thanking us for coming to his birthday party. He ended by saying, "Let's see if we can do what we talked about—getting together in the Caribbean or Florida sometime this spring or summer or fall. We'll just work at it and see if it can happen."

We were never able to take that vacation together, and Sam died almost exactly a year later.

chapter six

THE BIGGEST REGRET OF ALL

At the very moment when I should have felt like I was on top of the world, I felt like I had just awoken in the middle of a nightmare.

It is hard to explain how I made such a stupid mistake. It's hard for me to understand myself. What I did was dumb—really dumb, and I have never regretted anything more in my life.

Nonetheless, one of the reasons I wrote this book is so that others may learn by reading my story about my stupidity and appreciate the essence of what I had to learn the hard way: cutting corners can turn into something so big it puts everything else in your life at risk. I tell you my story with regret and remorse, and I'm sorry that I put my company, my customers, and my family through the nightmare. But, as surprising as it may sound, some good things came of it.

During an average week,100,000 people visited our store.

Our store had become so crowded with customers that the fire marshal told me we had far too many people inside. He cautioned me that if we didn't strictly follow the legal limit of occupancy, he would have to shut us down. To solve the problem, I hired a security guard to stand at the front door on busy weekends and not allow new shoppers to go inside until an equal number of shoppers came out. At the end of the afternoon rush, when the guard was no longer needed, I simply went over to one of my cash registers and paid him in cash. I was always busy and never gave it much thought.

In addition to the fire marshal's ruling, it was obvious to

us that no customer ever likes to wait in line to check out. As the store got busier, it became clear that I needed a bigger store!

With ten checkout stands instead of three, we could check out our customers faster and no one would have to wait in line. I calculated the amount of extra space we would need to add seven more cash registers and sketched a plan. I saw that we could easily push out a wall to enlarge our retail sales area at the same time, but the wall was where the big refrigerator was, so we would have to move the refrigerator back. That would give us more refrigerator space for the increasing number of products we could sell.

All of this would cost money, which, unfortunately, I didn't have. I had already borrowed all the money from my bank that was possible, considering the original cost overruns that I incurred when I built the store. There was simply no way that I could borrow another penny until my sales grew substantially. Of course, that wouldn't be possible until I enlarged my store. It was a classic Catch-22 situation: until I could add more products to my store, I couldn't generate more profits, but I couldn't generate more profits until I added onto the store.

WOW! What a Deal!

Then one day, I was standing in our parking lot with a friend who was a contractor. His construction crew was expanding our parking lot with fresh asphalt. As the crew poured and smoothed the black tar and gravel, my friend said something that stopped me in my tracks.

"Stew, would there be any chance that you could pay me for this job in cash? If you could, I would be willing to give you a 20 percent discount."

A 20 percent discount? Just for paying in cash? Why, almost every sale we made was in cash. Of course I could handle that. I could just take the cash from one of my own registers (I'd have to slow down on paying my other bills for a few weeks), put the cash aside, and pay for the work when it was completed. Plus, I'd get a 20 percent discount. What a deal!

A couple of weeks later, I asked my contractor friend if he would consider making me the same deal if I wanted to expand my store.

"No problem!" he said. At the time, I didn't consider the IRS consequences of such an idea. The furthest thing from my mind was that I might end up in jail for cutting corners in order to enlarge my store. After all, I rationalized I owned a business and was paying for the work from my own cash registers, with my own money. I simply took the cash I needed each week to pay the contractors and put it into a safe in my office. I began to call the money "The Building Fund."

With the building enlarged, lots of additional new space at the front of the store, and seven new cash registers to speed things up, our sales continued to grow. Still, I had one big problem: every month I came up short and had to struggle to pay my bills. Yet that first addition and the increased sales it generated went a long way toward helping me get on solid ground. If I could put on one more addition, I would have space to increase my product line even more. With Mrs. Schultze's property next door, we had the land to expand, so I began work with Dick Bergmann to design the construction plans for an even bigger store. Everything seemed to be coming together nicely.

Planning for the Future

I was quickly approaching my fiftieth birthday—just eight years away from the age my father had been when he had his third and final heart attack. When my Dad died, he left his affairs unsettled, and it caused a lot of estate problems; he had left no will or succession plan. I realized that if I didn't want to repeat that mistake, I needed to create an estate plan for my family.

My friend Bernie Gouz recommended a lawyer from New York who was an expert on taxes and planning. I met with him and we hit it off right away. He was streetsmart, and he joined our team as our legal adviser. I had a long list of things for him to help me with: estate planning, the succession of the business to our children, accounting, and other issues.

One day I confided in him that I was setting aside some cash each week for my building fund. I realized that what I was doing was wrong and I wanted to stop, but I didn't know how to stop it without sending up red flags. It was like riding a tiger: easier to get on than to get off.

My attorney seemed unconcerned.

"You're not doing anything that lots of other entrepreneurs don't do," he said.

"But what would happen if I got audited by the IRS and my building fund was discovered?" I asked.

"You would probably be fined heavily by the IRS, and they would make you pay all of your back taxes, plus interest and penalties," he said. The building fund was making the difference between struggle and success, so it seemed like it was worth the risk. Of course, I rationalized, it was only a temporary situation.

I had always intended that the building fund be a temporary stopgap measure to just help me get past my early growing pains. I would discontinue it as soon as I finished this one last addition. As I think back on it now, I am amazed at how shortsighted and naive I was. It reminds me of the old saying, "It's easier to refuse the first peanut than the second."

The business was operating smoothly. Our managers had taken over purchasing and the day-to-day operations, Stew Jr. had become our president, busy with personnel management as well as buying, advertising, and merchandising, and Tom was busy with our new farmers' market in Danbury. I could see my dream of finally slowing down and taking some time off becoming a reality. My sixtieth birthday neared. With my lessened workload, I would be able to focus my attention on the things I loved to do, like giving keynote speeches and promoting our business at industry conventions.

The Inevitable Finally Happens

Early one August morning in 1991, seven IRS agents showed up at our offices. They came up the silo stairs and into our reception area and asked to see me. I wasn't there yet, so Helynn, the receptionist, called Jill, who was always in early. She put them in the conference room, offered them coffee, and called me from her office.

"Okay, Jill, thanks. I'll be right there," I said and hung up the phone. We weren't expecting a visit from the IRS, but I had a sick feeling that I knew exactly why they were there. The agents had search warrants for our offices, and they spent several hours filling their vans with the contents of our file cabinets. They also took away several computers. I was later astonished to discover that the information they built their case on was not what they found in my office. A disgruntled former employee, a security guard who knew about the building fund, provided it.

When the IRS launched its investigation, I expected to have to pay some back taxes, and I knew that the fines and penalties would be quite stiff. My attorney advised us to hire attorneys who specialized in IRS cases of this sort. The new firm studied the facts of our case and immediately gave me some horrific news: I would definitely not be allowed to simply pay the back taxes and fines on the underreported income. The laws had changed, and while in the past, judges had had discretion in sentencing and could waive a jail sentence for a white-collar crime, these days there were federal sentencing guidelines, and they included incarceration along with the penalties and fines.

It soon became apparent that the IRS was a brutally tough adversary. And to make matters worse, my high profile made me a desirable target, a case that the IRS could publicize as a strong deterrent to others who might be tempted to underreport their income. The U.S. attorney's office came down on me very hard. They interviewed everyone and investigated every lead.

After two full years of investigation, in the spring of 1993, my attorneys were called to a meeting at the U.S. attorney's offices in New Haven. After negotiations that went on late into the day, they finally brought me the results. The government's proposition was simple: if I did not plead guilty, they would attack everyone in my family, including Marianne, who had innocently signed all our tax returns, and Stew Jr., whose guilt they would attempt to prove because he held the title of president of our company. But if I pleaded guilty and accepted full responsibility, they would only charge me, not my family. It would all be over. My attorneys waited for my decision.

"There's nothing further to discuss," I said. I would never let my family be attacked for something I had done. By doing something that I deeply regretted, I had jeopardized the livelihood of everyone associated with Stew Leonard's. I knew what I had to do: face the music and take full responsibility. That responsibility weighed heavily on me, and it is impossible to describe the remorse that I felt.

My attorneys called the U.S. Attorney's office the next morning and said that I would agree to the offer.

Paying the Piper

In July 1993, with my family by my side, I appeared at the federal courthouse in New Haven. The first couple of rows in the courtroom were filled with my family: Marianne; Stew Jr. and Tom and their wives; Jill and Beth and their husbands; my brother Leo; and my sisters Dot and Anna Lane. I was still recovering from a recent hip replacement operation and from open-heart and valve replacement surgery that I'd undergone in anticipation of a probable prison sentence.

How much of my poor health could be attributed to the stress that I'd battled since the IRS investigation started, from the legal bills that were piling up and from the shame for what I'd done, I can't say. But when I got to court that day, I was no longer the robust, happy man I'd been all my life. I looked and felt old, and my health was fragile.

I stood before the judge and entered my guilty plea to the charges against me. The judge lectured me, stating that underpaying income taxes is a very serious crime and that if everyone would pay all they owed to the IRS, we would be able to eliminate the national debt. He took this opportunity to make an example out of me in front of the media that packed the courtroom.

I was sentenced to fifty-two months in a minimum-security federal prison camp. I was ordered to pay full restitution of all unpaid taxes, heavy fines and the interest, which equalled to more than twice the taxes I owed, and for my incarceration and court costs.

As I stood before the court, filled with remorse, I deeply regretted what I had done. I knew that I had no one to blame but myself, I knew what I had done was wrong and that I deserved all the penalties that the judge was handing out to me. It is a regret that I will carry with me for the rest of my life. As a final part of the sentence, the judge imposed 704 hours of community service. Because my attorneys had stressed my poor health, the judge decided that I should not immediately be sent to a federal camp, but instead ordered me to first report to the federal medical prison in Rochester, Minnesota on November 29 for medical evaluation.

I was not looking forward to going away, and I knew that I had to prepare myself mentally. To get ready for what I knew would be a demoralizing and horrible experience, I read one of the greatest books ever written, *Man's Search for Meaning* by Viktor Frankl. Frankl had been imprisoned in a Nazi concentration camp during World War II. He wrote that the most important thing one has to do when facing incarceration is to get your mind-set correct. He believed that by controlling the way you think and keeping your thoughts positive, you could get through any experience, even being in the most dehumanizing place in the world, as he was.

Frankl's book also made me realize that I was lucky. No matter how difficult and demeaning my incarceration might be, it would be nothing compared to what he went through. I was grateful for his book, and I steeled myself for the next four years of my life.

It Was Worse than I Thought It Would Be

On November 28, 1993, a cold, rainy Sunday right after Thanksgiving, I left the warm comfort of our home in Connecticut to fly to Minnesota to begin my sentence. It was one of the saddest days of my life. I hugged Jill, Beth, and Marianne good-bye and drove with Stew Jr. and Tom to Kennedy Airport.

I soon realized that my attorneys, in requesting that I be sent to a medical facility due to my health, made a major mistake: the judge had ordered that I be sent to a high-security institution.

The Rochester medical center was a general-population prison, a compound surrounded by barbed wire and, armed guards. It housed inmates from all over the country who needed medical attention that they would receive at the nearby Mayo Clinic. The inmates at Rochester weren't just the white-collar types that my attorneys thought I would be with; there were murderers, rapists, and drug dealers, too. When they were taken to the Mayo Clinic for treatment, they went in orange jumpsuits and shackles, accompanied by two guards.

After I was checked in, I was taken to the "dorm" where I would sleep. It was a large cinder-block room overcrowded with beds filling the room from one end to the other, each bed touching the one next to it, There is an old prisoner's adage that says "The first night in prison you sleep like a baby: you wake up every hour on the hour and cry!" Well, it wasn't quite that bad, but the noise was constant, the lights were never turned off, and people talked and snored loudly all night. It was impossible to sleep.

During the day, everyone was under lockdown. The men just sat on their beds, waiting for a work assignment or a doctor's appointment. Eventually everyone was assigned a job to do. Mine was to empty the trash cans filled with inmates' needles and bandages.

I quickly learned the rules of conduct: keep your head down and your mouth shut. Do not look anyone in the eye or confide in him. Walk, never run, and do exactly what you are told. One of the highlights for some of the men was visiting with their families on weekends. Inmates had to wear orange jumpsuits, and visitors were searched. Rochester was such a humiliating, depressing place that I never wanted my family to visit.

Although I was safe at Rochester and no one harmed me, I was afraid every day that the horror stories of prison life might come true. There was nothing like a place like Rochester to convince me that my health was fine. My son Tom worked diligently with my lawyers to request a transfer to a federal prison camp as soon as possible.

"You're Here as Punishment, Not For The Punishment."

—WARDEN DENNIS LUTHER

Just before Christmas, on December 23, I was summoned by one of the head guards. I was taken to the office and given the news I had been praying for—the doctors had given me a medical okay and I was being transferred. It was a bitter-cold, 19-degrees-below-zero Minnesota morning, and even though I had nothing to wear but my khaki pants and shirt, I was thrilled to be leaving Rochester! Two armed guards placed me in shackles and drove me in a prison vehicle to the airport. I was put on a transport plane and sent to Bradford, Pennsylvania. From the airport there, I was taken to the minimum-security federal prison camp, McKean Federal Correctional Institution, in north-central Pennsylvania.

When we arrived at McKean, I couldn't believe my eyes. There were no barbed-wire fences, no armed guards, no towers, not even a fence around the camp. There was just a mark at the end of the sidewalk that meant you couldn't walk any further! The camp was about a half mile away from the medium-security prison, with its armed guards and barbed wire fences that adjoined it. The McKean Camp was the opposite end of the spectrum from Rochester. It looked more like a community college than a prison camp, a series of square cinder-block buildings nestled among the trees. There was even a track where the inmates were allowed to walk for daily exercise.

I knew that I was fortunate to finally be at a camp with other nonviolent, white-collar men, many of whom were contractors and businessmen, former judges, or politicians. But my good fortune wasn't just in being among low-risk inmates; it was being in the finest, best-run facility in the entire U.S. Bureau of Prisons system.

But make no mistake about it, for all of its appearance as a more civilized place, McKean was still a federal prison camp, and the guards enjoyed exercising their power over the inmates. The day I arrived, I got there late in the afternoon. The guard who had escorted me to my cube told me that dinner was almost over, and that if I wanted to eat I'd better hurry to the mess hall. He pointed the way and I began to walk quickly, but when I heard the bell signaling the end of dinner, I broke into a jog. A guard stopped me, pointed to a sign on the wall that read "No Running," and told me to go back to my dorm building and then walk to the mess hall. By the time I made the 300-yard walk, I'd missed dinner, and I hadn't eaten since dinner the night before. It was my first lesson that McKean was really just like any other prison, not the cushy "Club Fed" minimum-security prisons were rumored to be.

Among the things inmates are deprived of is sleep, and it's a difficult thing to get used to. The lights and the television are never turned off. The only quiet time each day was those last few hours before dawn. I quickly fell into a routine of getting up at five each morning and watching the sunrise over the Endless Mountains, as the range that surrounded Bradford was called. Breakfast wasn't served until 6:30; so every day I would spend that time thinking of the world outside, of my family, and of all of the things that I was grateful for. To boost my attitude each morning, I would sing a little song to myself, to the tune of the Disney song "Hi-Ho, Hi-Ho":

Hoo-ray, hoo-ray,
I feel great today.
Something good will come my way,
Hoo-ray, hoo-ray, hoo-ray, hoo-ray...

To help me focus on the positive things in my life, I put together a binder called *My What's Good Book.* It was filled with positive quotes and stories, humorous things that had happened that day, lists of any accomplishments, things I was grateful for, things I'd like to do when I got home, things I dreamed of doing. I had photographs of my family and friends, and I looked at the pictures over and over again until the pages became torn and tattered. I depended on this book to make me smile and give me comfort. Every day I would write in the book about some good things that happened that day. I always was able to write something regardless of how simple a thing it was: I received a letter from home, we had chicken for dinner, only three more days until winter officially ends, and so on. I knew that unless I continued looking for the good and focusing on the positive, prison would wear me down the way it had so many of the other guys.

I also made a list of tips to remind me how to best get through my time. One of the things I wrote was this little poem to Marianne:

> *When we're on the telephone,*
> *You may think we're all alone.*
> *But someone else that we can't see,*
> *Is listening to you and me.*
> *So please don't ever bare your soul*
> *Or I might end up in the hole!*

And I made lists of other advice like: "Leave the 'woulda, shoulda, couldas' at home." "What's over is over." "'Tis little good you'll do watering last year's crops." And, most important: "Don't ever tell your family anything bad that happened to you." I felt that our families had it far worse than we did, so it was important to keep their spirits up by talking only about positive things. It used to really bother me when I'd overhear some guy on the phone, complaining about some inconvenience, when his poor wife on the other end of the phone probably was suffering more than he was.

The highlight of each week was visiting day. I would look forward to it all week, because when I got to the visitors' center on Saturday morning, Marianne would be waiting for me.

I was one of the fortunate ones at camp; I saw Marianne almost every weekend and my children and other family and friends quite frequently. Bradford was a long way from Westport—a seven-hour drive each way—but Tom, who had earned his pilot's license, bought a secondhand Mooney Acclaim so that he could fly Marianne to Bradford every weekend. If he couldn't stay for the weekend, he would fly her up on Saturday, then come back for her Sunday afternoon. Marianne and many of the other visiting wives stayed nearby where they shared meals and got to know each other. Saturday and Sunday mornings they would stand in line, be

While at federal prison camp, the highlight of each week was a visit from Marianne. Her optimism and attitude helped to keep my spirits up.

searched, and then go into the visiting room to wait for their loved ones.

While it was humiliating that my stupidity made it necessary for all my visitors to be searched before they could see me, I felt very lucky that my family and so many of my friends made the long trip. One time my friend Graeme Alford even flew all the way from Australia to pay a visit, which I deeply appreciated. There were lots of poor souls whose family or friends rarely came to see them, and many inmates had no visitors at all. I knew several fellows who didn't get to see their children at all while they were away at camp, and many marriages broke up.

While Saturdays were the best, Sundays, after the visitors left, were the worst. The fellows used to say they suffered from what they called PVD—"post-visit depression." After visiting hours were over, we'd all go back to our cubes and lie quietly on our beds, depressed and filled with sadness.

Camp also compounds personal tragedies. One day Marianne called to tell me that my sister Marion had died. Of course I was not allowed to attend her funeral; it was another of the penalties that was a consequence of my stupid actions.

One Hand Washes the Other

While work is a part of every prison program, Warden Luther believed that making a contribution was important in rehabilitating inmates. Jobs at McKean ranged from the mundane, such as kitchen, landscaping, or janitorial assignments, to the skilled, such as teaching GED classes or working in the library.

Luther was right. In his assignment for me I found not only challenge, but also rewards in helping the local merchants with their business problems. The Bradford Merchants' Workshop gave me a purpose. I loved sharing the ideas and philosophies that had helped me and might help others. I loved thinking about the challenges that the Bradford merchants had and how I might assist them in seeing another way to do things that would improve their businesses. During the week, while I was scrubbing floors or washing dishes, I was lost in thoughts of what I could share with them on Wednesday when we met again. It was a fulfilling opportunity, to focus on helping someone else rather than immersing myself in self-pity.

As Glenn and I became more and more involved in working with the local merchants, my time at McKean began to pass more rapidly. That is, until Dennis Luther announced that he was retiring. We soon realized that our progressive little corner of the prison world was an anomaly. While Luther had been the star of the penal system in the outside world, celebrated in magazine articles and in Tom Peters's books, many people inside the system disagreed with his methods, and many were envious of all of the attention he was receiving. The prevailing school of thought at the Bureau of Prisons was that inmates needed to be punished and that nothing about prison should be positive or constructive.

The new warden at McKean obviously disliked the role I had in helping the local business community. He didn't see why any inmate should be assisting the outside population, and he certainly didn't like the fact that the local townspeople were conducting weekly workshops on prison grounds. He quickly identified me as someone who needed to be put in his place, and as soon as he became warden, I was reassigned to a job in the kitchen, and the Bradford Merchants' Workshop was eliminated for good.

A few weeks after he became warden, I was awakened at 2 a.m. by a flashlight shining in my face. Two guards from the prison barked to me that I had two minutes to get up and get dressed. They took me over to the main prison, and with no explanation, I was shipped to Federal Correction Institution Schuylkill, a prison camp in Minersville, Pennsylvania, near Philadelphia. I was not allowed to speak on the phone to my family or have visitors for six months; letters were the only way I was allowed to communicate with my family. Fortunately, Glenn had heard what had happened, and he called Marianne the next day to tell her I'd been transferred. He felt he was probably going to be next.

At Schuylkill, the work was much more structured and the camp was overcrowded. I was assigned a bunk in the TV room, and for the first week, that was where I waited all day every day for the duty officer to assign me a job. Finally he got to me and asked what I'd done in the past. I told him I had been a milkman, and he thought that was like working on a farm, so he assigned me to the greenhouse.

The greenhouse was like a separate world. While my bunk was in the middle of the loud, often rowdy TV room, the greenhouse was quiet and warm. It was a sanctuary where I spent as much time as I was allowed, often volunteering for extra duties on weekends and holidays. It was a walk of several hundred yards down the hill from camp, but I made the walk there two or three times a day—in the morning, then again after lunch, and sometimes even after dinner. I took great pride in growing plants and flowers for the institution, and no one bothered me except the camp guards as they made their rounds.

After dinner, we sometimes were allowed to attend a movie screening. One series offered was Ken Burns's *The Civil War.* One of the stories was about a soldier named Sullivan Ballou, who wrote to his wife the night before the Battle of Bull Run. In his letter, he tells of his commitment to his cause and country, and he contemplates the possibility of death. The next day was his very first battle, and he was killed. The story was a chilling reminder that as unpleasant as my situation might become at times, it was nothing compared to what soldiers lived through so that they could fight for their country. I thought of my own two brothers, Leo and Jim, both going off to war, being shot at, with the possibility of being captured by the enemy, or maybe never coming home.

As much as I hated being in camp, I was grateful every day that I was safe. I kept reminding myself of the advice my friend Danny Cox gave me before I left home: "When there is no choice, be brave."

The days ground on, slowly turning into weeks, the weeks into months, and the months into years. Finally, my release date was set. My friends Neil and Ruthven surprised me with a big farewell party in the recreation room. It was a dress-up affair, by prison standards. My fellow inmates and I all wore white t-shirts with black bow ties drawn on them in magic marker, so we looked as if we were at a formal affair in tuxedos. Some of the guys had saved up their commissary supply allotments to put together snacks to go with our Cokes and Pepsis. Lots of friends gave toasts and roasted me. One of the fellows even wrote a song, which they all sang.

Double Fines and Double Penalties

During the party, Neil wanted me to say a few words. He asked, "Stew, how about telling us all what you learned from this prison experience?"

I thought about it carefully and replied:

"First off, I know that I did something wrong and I regret it with all of my heart. I built a business on doing things the right way and when I made the choice to do things the wrong way, I ended up with a prison sentence, double fines, and double penalties.

"The other day, I wrote a little poem to myself for *My What's Good Book*.

I did the things I had to do,
It taxed me through and through.
But looking back in retrospect,
I'm now a stronger Stew.

"Surprisingly, my time in prison was not all bad. I learned you can make up for any mistake if you extract the misdeed and vow to never repeat it again. I found ways to help people and that helped me through my experience. I came to appreciate my wife and my family even more. And I discovered that there are a lot of things I want to do in life and I am going to get busy doing them, because life is a lot shorter than we think.

"I will arrive home in much better health and physical shape than I was in when I began my sentence.

"I also have decided that when I get home, I am not going to go back to my old job of running the business, with its eighteen-hour days. Instead, I am going to hand over the reins to my children and spend more time with Marianne at our home on St. Martin."

Finally, in April 1997, after forty-two months of incarceration, I was released, and Marianne and I drove back to Connecticut.

Yellow Ribbons

When we pulled into the driveway, there were yellow ribbons tied around every tree in the yard,and Beth and Jill were holding a huge banner that said "Welcome Home." Stew Jr., Kim, Tom, Rocky, Karen, and Bill were all waiting to greet me.

To see my family waiting for me was the most rewarding feeling in the world: I had paid my dues, it was over, and I could move on. It was a real reason to celebrate.

Inside the house, our children and grandchildren had set up a celebration party. It was just our family, and for a moment it felt as if nothing had changed, that things were just like they had been before. But later that night, after everyone left and the house was quiet, I couldn't sleep. My own bed felt strange and unfamiliar. The house was dark and quiet. When I got up in the middle of the night to go to the bathroom, I bumped into the furniture. My old familiar surroundings had become unfamiliar. It would take me several more nights to get used to being home again.

My probation was conditioned on six months of home confinement. Even though home confinement rules allowed me to go to work, I didn't feel like going in to my store; I didn't know what to expect. But one day I decided to bite

On arriving home from prison camp, I was greeted with yellow ribbons, a "Welcome Home" banner, and my entire family.

the bullet and go to say hello to some of the customers and Team Members. I stood at the front door, greeting customers as they entered. It was great shaking hands and saying hello to all of my old friends. Then I walked through the store, working backward through the flow of customers, which was the best way to see their faces, because they were all heading toward me. They were all smiling and happy to see me, patting me on the back and welcoming me home. It was just as if I had never left, and it sure felt great to be back!

chapter seven

BUILDING TEAM ONE

Early one cold November Saturday, just before my little dairy store's grand opening, I put on my coat, got in my car, and headed over to the store. As I pulled up to a traffic light, I heard a shuffling sound from the backseat. I stopped the car and looked back to find little Jill, just eight years old, hiding on the floor behind the driver's seat.

"What are you doing there, honey?" I asked.

"I want to go to work with you, Dad," Jill said, a huge grin on her face for having hidden successfully in the car.

My first thought was to turn around and take her home, but then I thought to myself, what the heck, I'd helped my father when I was Jill's age. So I let her come. When I got to the store, I called Marianne to tell her what had happened.

"Well, that's going to cause problems," Marianne said.

Before I could ask why, she continued, "The other children will be jealous. They want to come to the store with you, too."

Pretty soon, the rest of my family pulled up in the parking lot, came inside, and got to work helping with all the little jobs that needed to be done to get the store ready for our grand opening. For the next two weekends, working together at our new store was a family event. The kids felt that they were an important part of it and came to help me whenever they could.

Finally, on the day before Thanksgiving, we were almost ready to begin processing milk. We started up the plant and had a trial run at packaging. Barry Bellardinelli, who had been the route supervisor at Clover Farms for many years, was now our store manager, and Ray Flewellyn and his son, Ray Jr., both of whom had managed our milk plant on Catherine Street, were in charge of our new dairy operations. They were all busy, with technicians and electricians making the final adjustments to our new, state-of-the-art systems. Finally, just before midnight, they gave the all-clear signal and began processing milk.

Marianne and I; our four children; my sisters Dot and Anna Lane; Barry and his wife, Eve; and my brother Leo climbed the stairs to the balcony that overlooked the milk plant. We stood there in awe, watching the first case of half-gallon cartons of milk roll off the conveyor belt. We uncorked a bottle of Champagne and toasted a new era for Clover Farms Dairy.

The Art of Passing the Baton

It was great fun having the children working with me as we readied the store for our grand opening. They loved pitching in and doing small jobs, and when the store opened, they were just as proud as I was. I soon realized that our new dairy store was going to become my new home away from home. So as long as I was going to have be there Saturdays, Sundays, and holidays, the best way for me to spend time with my family was to have them at the store with me.

My brother Leo, Bernie Gouz, and Joe Shaw provided me with great guidance in setting up the dairy store in those

Stew, Jr., Tom, Beth, Jill, Marianne, and I pose for our annual holiday card.

early days, but now I knew that I needed advice in creating a true family business. I found a wonderful little book, *Beyond Survival: A Business Owner's Guide for Success*, written by Dr. Léon Danco, founder of the Center for Family Business in Cleveland, Ohio. Dr. Danco stressed that the best way to make sure your children never want to go into your family business is for you to come home every night and complain about it during dinner. He said that as a business owner, you can't do worse than sit at the dinner table with your children listening to every word and talk about your bone-headed suppliers, your cranky customers, and your difficult employees. Because when your children get to be nineteen years old and you say to them, "Someday this will all be yours," they are going to say, "No thank you, Dad."

Marianne and I both hoped that our children would someday choose to work in the family business, and I knew that they would be more likely to want to if it was fun for them just like it had been for me. So every night, I told them exciting stories of the events of the day. Even if things hadn't been all that great that day, I at least was able to make it sound like fun: the chickens getting loose on Route 1, a huge display of cereal boxes falling like dominoes, the new baby calf we had just added to our little farm, the children's friends I'd seen in the store that day. Each night they waited to hear my stories, the excitement, and the news. I tried to create a picture of a happy place so that Stew Jr., Tom, Beth, and Jill would want to come to work with me whenever they could.

The year we opened, Stew was fifteen and Tom was thirteen. Finding jobs for them was easy because they were at just the right age and strength to lift cases of milk and juice and stock the shelves and coolers. They even earned extra change by pitching in to help the men unload the trucks and stack the milk cases. Beth and Jill soon became crackerjacks at operating the cash registers, though they had to stand on empty milk crates to reach the cash register keys. They were happy girls and a perfect complement to our store, even if they were a bit young at just eight and eleven years old. One day as Jill rang up a woman's purchase, the woman looked at her skeptically and said, "Aren't you a little young to be working here?"

Jill looked surprised at the question and just pointed to me, and said, "But my dad said it was okay!"

In 1973, when the store was just four years old, Stew left for Ithaca, New York, to study at Ithaca College. In his freshman year, he joined the lightweight crew team. He was quite a dedicated rower, eventually making captain of the varsity team during his senior year and leading his team to a bronze medal at the Dad Vail Regatta in Philadelphia, the first national title Ithaca's crew team had ever won.

But at his graduation, he delivered a bit of news that almost broke my heart: he said he had been recruited by Price Waterhouse, the big accounting firm, and wanted to work for them instead of working in the family business. We soon got over our disappointment, though, and Marianne and I were proud as punch over his graduation. The first one of our children to graduate from college! As a graduation present, we went a little overboard and presented him with a ticket on Pan Am Flight 002, a round-the-world tour. At $2,500 just for the airline ticket alone, it was an expensive gift, but it turned out to be a wonderful investment.

With a buddy from college, Stew took the summer off to see the world. On one of the flights, from Katmandu to Cairo, he sat next to an Indian businessman. The fellow proudly told Stew all about his family business that went back several generations. Stew told him about ours, but he said that he had chosen not to follow in my footsteps. The fellow was convinced that Stew was making a mistake. It was an honor to work for a family business, he said; he was a member of the fifth generation of his, and he was very proud of that.

"You should learn from your father, help to build the business instead of someone else's," the fellow said.

Walking off the plane, Stew began to have second thoughts. And later that same day, he called us from Cairo to tell us that he had told Price Waterhouse he had changed his mind. He was going to make a career at Stew Leonards!

A Little Bit of France—In Norwalk, Connecticut

After high school, Beth attended Skidmore College and then decided to earn her master's degree at Middlebury College, where she studied French and literature. One semester, she attended the Sorbonne in Paris.

After graduating from Ithaca College, Stew joined me at the dairy. I put his desk right next to mine so he could learn the business. Here, he introduces us to our first IBM computer.

She lived with a French family, and each day the mother spent hours cooking for her family, making everything from scratch. Beth loved to help out and to learn the French way of shopping and preparing meals. Every day the woman sent Beth to the renowned bakery Boulangerie Poilâne. Beth was amazed at the choices, the artistry, and the mouth-watering offerings. She fell in love with the way the French thought about food and how meals were a central part of each day, and she became intrigued by the bakery and cheese shops she visited throughout Paris.

When it was time to propose her master's thesis, Beth came up with something previously unheard of: a study of the business of cheese importing. Although her professors took some convincing, they finally agreed, and Beth spent much of the semester touring the French countryside interviewing cheese makers, exporters, and cheese shop owners.

Then, while she was working on her college thesis, Beth saw an opportunity. Cheese importing involved layers and layers of middlemen, each one adding to the cost, but she thought it would be possible to cut out the middlemen and pass the savings on to our customers back home in Connecticut. She called and explained what she had learned, the opportunity she saw for us, and what it would take to set up our own importing operation. She could make arrangements for us to import cheese directly from France at half the cost of buying through distributors. Would I allow her to give it a try? You bet I would!

How could I say no? I was excited because it meant that Beth would join the family business after her graduation. We set up a telex machine to place and confirm our orders, and we built large display cases. Beth worked to get our cheese operation underway, and soon we announced, with a huge sign over our front door, "Brie Imported from France, 40 Percent Off!" We set up tables with free samples and sales took off. Soon Beth had to expand, also buying cheese from Wisconsin. Best of all, the cheese business was a natural for our dairy-store image.

One day Beth received a call from a college friend who had moved to Washington, D.C., and whose days were filled with exciting jobs and evenings packed with social engagements. She invited Beth to join her. Beth sat down with me and explained that she wanted to join her college roommate and look for a job in Washington. Naturally, I didn't want to hold her back, and I realized that our little store could not compete with all the excitement Washington had to offer.

Beth left to look for a job, and while she was away, we received a phone call for her. Marianne called Beth in Washington and relayed the message: the regional head of Vie de France, a French baking company, wanted to see if she might be interested in taking a job with them. The company had developed a baking system that allowed authentic French croissants, relatively unheard of in America at the time, to be frozen for shipment and then baked fresh daily in the store. They were looking for a sales representative to sell the concept to American supermarkets.

"Dad," Beth said, "what would you think if I came back to the store and we sold croissants?"

"I would be as happy as a lark, honey! By the way, what are croissants?"

Beth called Vie de France and told them she couldn't take the management position but that she would be interested in becoming one of their customers. She set up one of their systems at our store, and she soon began baking croissants. The aroma of the buttery, fresh-baked, hot-out-of-the-oven rolls filled the store, and she could hardly keep up with the demand. Customers were breaking into their bags to sample them right in the store while they were shopping.

The Vie de France croissants renewed a passion for baking in Beth. She suggested that we build our own in-store bakery so instead of selling store-baked frozen croissants, we could make and bake our own product from scratch. We both agreed that if Beth was serious about operating her own French bakery, she should return to Paris and study with expert French bakers. We enlisted the help of Roy Halstead, a consultant on European methods of marketing products, and he opened the doors to French baking for us.

When Beth returned home, she was filled with ideas and ideals, and croissants were just the beginning. She insisted that we should make everything from scratch. Our products would taste better and be of the highest quality; we wouldn't even need preservatives. And our product line could respond to customer's desires. Bran muffins in addition to blueberry? Whole-grain breads in addition to white? Bagels in addition to croissants? She could bake them all. And we could make everything fresh every day.

At the time, most supermarket chains were heading in the opposite direction. They were reducing costs by switching their scratch bakeries over to frozen bake-off departments, which were much less expensive to operate.

Our new bakery was built onto the front of the store and was the first department customers came to when they entered. They were hit with the scent of baking breads and the aroma of cinnamon rolls. It was almost irresistible. Bakery sales reached $50,000 a week within the first year. Eventually "Bethy's Bakery," according to the Food Marketing

"Bethy's Bakery" quickly became one of the largest in-store bakeries in the United States.

Institute, became one of the largest in-store bakeries in the country.

From MBWA to MBA

Shortly after Beth left to pursue her master's degree, Stew Jr. decided that he wanted to learn more, too. He had been working alongside me since he graduated from Ithaca. We had set up a desk for him right in my office so that he would be able to be in on the product-buying as well as the people-management ends of the business. In the two years since he'd graduated, he'd been an enormous help in improving our organization.

Stew discovered that we lacked a long-term strategy. When it came to running our store, I simply made lists of projects that needed to be done, and then we did them. He felt we needed more structure and long-range planning. He thought being able to look at year-to-year comparable data for each department could help our people do their jobs better. He said long-range planning would improve our ability to manage our resources and increase our sales, and that feedback from department managers would help us to see where we could improve our products and systems. He also thought we needed to formalize our communication through regular meetings, which would allow news and ideas to be shared and frustrations to be vented.

Our interviewing process needed improvement too, he said, and our training processes were too informal. When we suddenly became the target of a unionization attempt, it pitted our front-end people against our managers, and we had to scramble to keep everyone happy.

Stew also knew that we would need more professional management at some point. He hoped to be the one to fill that role: his solution was to go back to school and earn a master's in business administration.

At first, I wasn't very eager to think of him leaving the business for two whole years. I was confident that as smart and capable as he was, he could figure out how to do what

Stew Jr. graduating from the University of California, Los Angeles with an MBA.

he thought we needed to do while still working at my side. But Stew was convinced; I was the one who would have to change my mind.

After looking at MBA programs at several schools, he decided to apply to the University of California at Los Angeles. UCLA emphasized something the other colleges he looked at hadn't: people. Their more progressive philosophies were based on the Japanese style of management, and the idea of learning how to grow people rather than just work with numbers appealed to Stew. In the fall of 1980, he left for L.A.

Too Many Chiefs, Not Enough Stores

By the summer of 1982, all our children were falling into step in our business. Stew Jr. had graduated from UCLA and come back to work at the store, and he was engaged to his college sweetheart, Kim Kral. Tom, after enrolling at the University of Denver, became engaged to his college sweetheart, Karen Lande, and they had moved back to Westport. Beth was busy running her new bakery, and Jill was preparing to head off for college in Boston; it was only a matter of a few short years before she would join us as well.

But it soon became apparent that, with their college educations, our children wanted more than simply stocking shelves and running cash registers. I was lucky that Beth had found her own passion, building her own bakery and cheese operations. With his MBA, Stew was on track to run the company someday. Which left Tom; it was my goal to help him find his own challenging niche within the business.

Tom, true to his character, returned from Denver with a bang. He came in and immediately used his creativity to add excitement to the store. He introduced the idea of audio-animatronics, similar to what we had seen at Disney World, which brought another WOW! to our store. Tom purchased farmer and cow animatronics, and "Sally at the Piano," which was a sensation.

While Tom thrived in an atmosphere that was open to spontaneity and filled with excitement, Stew's path was always deliberate and consistent. And both were right: we needed excitement, and we needed stability, too.

The business was continuing to grow and my brother Leo recommended that I ask business consultant Lee Snider, a former executive at Pepperidge Farms for advice.

Lee came to the store and studied every department. He took notes, counted cars and customers, and looked at sales receipts. Soon he gave me a twenty two-page report that came to one single conclusion: if we wanted to continue the kind of growth we had seen in the past, we needed to build a second store at a new location.

At first the idea didn't appeal to me. I'd spent more than a decade nurturing this one, and finally my older son was ready to take it over. Maybe it was time to relax and enjoy life. But the more I thought about the fact that I had two sons, the more I thought that maybe a second store wouldn't be such a bad idea after all.

One day, a longtime Team Member, Bruce Mathieson, mentioned to me that on his way to work every day he passed a forty-four-acre farm right on Federal Road in Danbury. It had a "For Sale" sign on it, he said. My brother-in-law Frank talked me into taking a look at the land with him. It was certainly an ideal location, and the fact that it was a rural farm made it perfect for us. Soon I began negotiating for the land, and before too long, we were the proud owners of a big tract of land that would eventually become our second location.

It would take a few years to navigate the permits and zoning approvals process in Danbury to get permission to build our store. So, month after month, we had to continue to make mortgage payments on a vacant piece of land.

"It's too bad we can't do anything with that wonderful property," Tom said. "Dad, do you think I could buy a few loads of Christmas trees and sell them there? After all, thousands of cars drive by that site every day."

Hmmm, I thought, that sounds like a good idea. One of the great things about Tom's idea was that customers would begin to become aware of the Stew Leonard name in Danbury.

Tom and his cousin Danny Arthur quickly had the lot filled with hundreds of Christmas trees leaning on stretched lines of wire. They put up a large red-and-white striped circus tent complete with Christmas lights and hung a Stew Leonard's banner across the front. They also sold greenery and wreaths, along with apple cider, and they even set up a sound system that played holiday music. The Christmas trees were a big hit, and soon Tommy and Danny had to order additional truckloads!

Tom became so enthusiastic that the next spring he put the tent up again and began selling plants and local fruits and vegetables. The next thing I knew, Tom and Danny were operating a full-fledged farmers' market under the tent year-round, with native corn in the summer; apples and pumpkins and cornstalks in the fall; Christmas trees in December; plants in the spring; and fruits and vegetables all year long. Tom and Dan nurtured the operation, adding items and improving their offerings whenever they could, until finally our approvals were final and we began construction of our new permanent store.

Tom thought it was important to maintain the tent until the store was open, so every day until it opened, he had two jobs: overseeing construction of the new store and making sure the tent operated smoothly. Finally, in the summer of 1991, we held the grand opening of our new store, with Tom as the proud new president.

Shortly after we opened the store, we received an incredible customer note:

"Dear Stew: I've been shopping in your Danbury Farmer's Market for a few months now and love it. However, every time I come in, I always see your son Tom working hard, but I rarely see you. Don't you think HIS picture should be up over the suggestion box instead of yours?"

It sounded like a good idea, so we sent a photographer up to the store to take Tom's picture. About a week later, I happened to show the note to Marianne. She looked at it and said, "Don't you recognize your own son's handwriting?"

Jill Fills the Bill

Ever since she was a little girl, Jill had spent her summers working at the store. Being the youngest, she worked as a cashier, at our customer service desk, handing out ice cream cones, and assisting in the bakery while her siblings took on bigger and bigger jobs in the store. All those years of working part-time made me realize that she loved working with people and had a knack for human relations.

Jill earned a degree in business administration from the University of San Diego, and she returned to Norwalk with her heart set on seeing herself at the helm of our human resources department. But her siblings thought differently. They insisted that their little sister prove her merit first.

The summer after she graduated, Jill joined us at our annual trip to the Food Marketing Institute Convention in Chicago. While we were there, Stew Jr., Tom, and Beth quizzed her continually: why did she want to work at the store? What could she contribute? What vision did she have for herself in the organization? As we spent the week learn-

Jill helped me with the business from the earliest days.

ing about all the new things being introduced in the food industry, we were also happy to learn of the determination and desire that Jill had to be a part of our family business.

When we returned from Chicago, Jill was hired to join our human resources team. However, since we already had a very talented and experienced head of HR, Karen Mazako, Jill was given a job as one of the department assistants, answering phones and filing paperwork. Bewildered but determined, she came to me. Stew, Tom, and Beth just got jobs at the store, she said, why did she have to start at the bottom of the ladder? Why were her brothers and sisters so hard on her?

"I know you want to be a big part of human resources someday," I said to her. "I could easily make you a manager in that department, and people would accept you because I said so. But if you work your way up from the bottom," I explained, "they will respect you because you earned it on your own."

Jill understood, and she quickly jumped in with both feet. She answered phones and took applications and helped Karen with interviewing, reviews, and training. She learned how every job was done and assisted wherever she was needed. Then one day, she was helping out with the payroll computer when by accident she wiped out the company's entire payroll history for the week. It was a huge and costly mistake. But it was a great learning experience. She had to go to every Team Member in the company and find out what their hours had been for that week. Finally, humbled and embarrassed, she came to me to tell me what had happened.

I sat quietly and listened. To her surprise, rather than becoming angry and critical, I told her a story about something that had once happened to me. When I was at the University of Connecticut, one of the requisites for graduation in the dairy manufacturing department was that each student take full responsibility for managing the university's dairy plant operation for a full week. During my tenure, one of the men working in the plant had forgotten to close the drain valve at the bottom of the big stainless steel milk tank that held the entire day's supply of milk, and all of the milk went right down into the sewer. I ended up getting the blame, because I was the plant manager that week.

The following day, Professor Dowd described the incident in front of the class and gave us a surprise quiz with just one question: "What should we do to the dairy plant worker who left the valve open?" Every single student in the class, including me, gave exactly the same answer: "Fire him!" We all received a zero on the quiz. Sixty years later, I still remember the lesson Professor Dowd taught us: It was an accident and accidents happen. Then I told Jill what Professor Dowd told us to learn from the incident:

"If you fire people who make a mistake and hire someone new, the new worker might make exactly the same mistake. But if you show the worker what was done wrong, and give him another chance, one thing is for sure: he will never make that same mistake again!"

Soon Jill and I took our first business trip together, to the Disney People management seminar at Disney World. Her eyes popped with amazement at the way all of the formal programs that Disney had in place made their operations seem so smooth and effortless. It was the essence of great human resources management.

When we returned to Connecticut, Jill was brimming over with ideas on how she could create an orientation program like the one we had just learned about at Disney. She believed that because of the constant turnover we had with high school students, a formal orientation program would better train our people, would better equip them to do their jobs, and would better position them for growth—they might even return to the company after college. Jill, just like Stew, Tom, and Beth, was beginning to bring a lot to the party by "blooming where she was planted."

The whole family with our diplomas from the Disney Management Seminar.

Not long afterward, Jill came to me with a brainstorm of her own. She was receiving telephone calls every week from corporations that wanted to send their management teams for tours of our operations for their managers. She pointed out that we had always appreciated the openness that other companies offered us when we asked to come see their business, and even the classroom format that Disney offered to anyone who wanted to sign up for their seminar.

"Dad, maybe we could start our own school and call it Stew Leonard's University?" I encouraged her and even enlisted the help of my good friend Danny Cox, an expert at planning seminars. Soon we were producing marketing materials and calling business magazines to promote Jill's new venture. For a small fee, companies could arrange a private four-hour tour and seminar with our management team. We would have some of our managers talk to them, explain our philosophy, and give a behind-the-scenes look at our operations. Stew Jr. or I were usually on hand and we were happy to answer questions. We even served them lunch!

Soon vanloads of executives were arriving at our store, usually wondering if their bosses were out of their minds sending them to a food store for people-management classes. But their skepticism didn't last long. At the end of the day, the executives left with lots of enthusiasm, big smiles, and ideas, all saying WOW! We quickly became a must-see operation for many Fortune 500 and blue chip companies. Executives from all over the country, and even from Japan and Europe, still come to get their "customer service diplomas" from Stew Leonard's University.

Over the years, Marianne and I had attended many seminars at Dr. Danco's Center for Family Business in Cleveland. He gave us advice on getting the children interested in working at the family business, bringing them into management without causing resentment in other managers, and building up respect for them among the rest of our team. Marianne and I always attended together with our children. We were apt students and couldn't wait to return home to put Dr. Danco's methods into action.

By the time I had turned sixty, with Stew Jr., Tom, Beth, and Jill all working with me, I had accomplished what I had long wanted to do: build a company on a foundation of customer service. Now it finally seemed like I was ready to take Dr. Danco's advice and transition the business to the next generation.

By 1991, our Norwalk store had been recognized by *The Guinness Book of World Records* as well as Ripley's Believe It or Not. And our newly opened store in Danbury was doing much more than we had hoped for. We had bridged a very crucial gap in our business—making the leap from one store to two.

chapter eight

FROM STRUGGLE COMES STRENGTH

One day in the summer of 1986, Stew Jr. suggested that Marianne and I come over for dinner with him, Kim, and their baby daughter Blake. At the table, Stew raised his glass in a toast.

"Dad, Mom, we have some news. Kim is pregnant!" Stew was exuberant. Then he added another stunning bit of news: "And it's going to be a boy. We've decided to name him Stew Leonard III."

I was practically speechless. And I was tremendously honored. The name Stew Leonard would continue to the third generation! That April, Kim gave birth to a beautiful healthy baby boy, Stewart John Leonard III. We called him Little Stewie.

By 1988, we had six grandchildren: Stew and Kim's Blake and Stewie; Tom and Karen's Tom Jr., who we called TJ, and daughter, Emma; Beth and Bill's daughter, Sarah; and Jill and Rocky's first son, Jake.

So it was with great happiness that we all gathered in St. Martin to celebrate the Christmas holidays that year. We would also be celebrating Blake's third birthday on New Year's Day.

Stew and Kim planned the birthday party, and our children and grandchildren spent the afternoon getting the house ready for the party, blowing up balloons and decorating. Kim was busy baking a birthday cake in the kitchen, and Stew and Tom were hanging up banners by the pool. Little Stewie was helping them. Suddenly Stew looked down from the ladder and didn't see his son. He immediately checked with Kim, but Stewie wasn't there either. Everybody began frantically searching, the house, the bedrooms, under the tables, out on the patio. Then, in a flash, before anyone knew what was happening, Stew dove into the pool and came up with little Stewie in his arms, his body limp and his eyes closed. For an instant, Stewie began to spit out water. Karen began CPR while Stew Jr. ran for the Jeep. He and Kim rushed Stewie to the hospital, praying for a miracle. The rest of the family got there as quickly as we could. As Marianne and I drove up to the hospital, we saw Stew and Kim sitting on a wall outside, shoulders hunched over, in shock and crying. The emergency room doctors were not able to revive Stewie. It was the saddest moment of our lives.

Soon Tom was by our side, and then Jill and Beth, who had come to the hospital to be with Stew and Kim. Afterward, we all returned to the house, heartbroken and asking ourselves why, how could this have happened? The pool deck was still decorated for the party, and a few of the balloons had drifted onto the surface of the pool. We realized that little Stewie must have fallen in reaching for one of the balloons. He was only twenty-one months old and still in diapers, and his diaper may have become waterlogged and pulled him to the bottom of the pool.

Our world was devastated. We all moved in slow motion, in shock, not knowing what to do next. Stew and Kim were in a daze, comforting each other, and Tom took on the difficult job of handling the arrangements. But since it was New Year's Day, all of the island's officials had the day off. Tom went to the police station, where he got the name

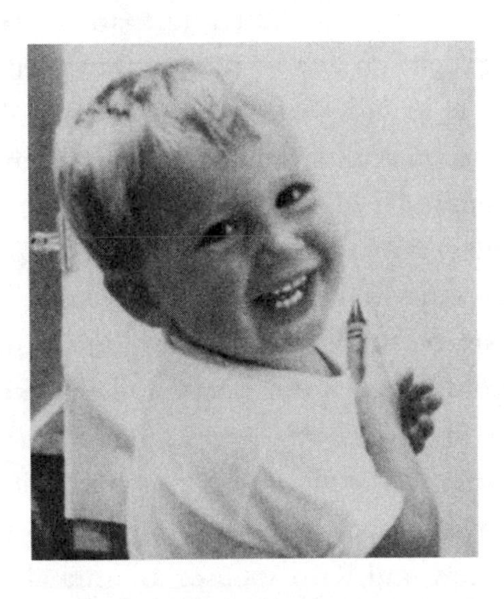

We lost our grandson, Stew Leonard III, at 21 months old.

of the Dutch funeral director and went to his home to beg him to open his office. Marianne called American Airlines, and although it was holiday weekend and all the flights were booked solid, the airline did the impossible and somehow reserved us all seats on the first flight home the following morning. It was a solemn trip for all of us, especially knowing that little Stewie was also making the trip home.

Stew and Kim's lives were shattered by their loss. Stew said that he felt that he might not ever recover from losing his son, and he didn't think they would ever have any more children. When Reverend Schuller heard the news, he called Stew from the Crystal Cathedral.

"This will color your life," Dr. Schuller said. "But it's up to you what color you choose."

As time went by, Stew and Kim began to realize that although losing their son was something they couldn't change, they could try to bring something positive out of the experience: to help prevent other children from drowning. In 1990, Stew and Kim established The Stew Leonard III Children's Charities. The charity's mission is to teach children to swim and to keep them safe in the water through education and training. To spread their message, Stew and Kim wrote two children's books about water safety and the importance of learning to swim: *Stewie the Duck Learns to Swim* and *Swimming Lessons with Stewie the Duck.* The foundation has raised millions of dollars to pay for swimming lessons for children. In addition, Stew and Kim sponsor an annual golf tourna-

Stew Jr. and Kim used their grief to help others. They created the Stew Leonard III Children's Charities, and authored two children's books on water safety. Here with good friend Martha Stewart after a segment on her television show (clockwise from left: Chase, Blake, Madison, Stew Jr., Kim, Martha, and Ryann).

ment and a water safety concert in Westport every spring to raise money for the foundation.

To boost awareness, they read their books to local schoolchildren and they began giving press interviews and appearing everywhere they could, including Martha Stewart's television program, *Today,* CBS News, and CNN, talking about their loss and the importance of water safety. The loss of Stewie was a tragedy but there is a silver lining: more than a hundred thousand children have learned to swim at YMCAs across the country thanks to Stew and Kim's efforts and the Stew Leonard III Foundation.

For Stew Jr. and Kim, it took a lot of strength and courage to move from devastation to helping others. I knew that Stew was smart and strong. He had always been one who looked for the deeper meaning, the hidden opportunity. So it was no surprise that in the face of this tragedy, and those that would be coming our way in the next few years, that he found the strength to turn the situations around by focusing on the positive instead of the negative.

Over the next few years, Tom, Beth, and Jill too would each learn to rise in the face of challenges and gain strength from the adversities they had to face. The next few years were a tough time for all of us, but we all eventually learned that it's not what happens to you that counts, it's what you do about it.

All of our children had to call on that strength the day the IRS showed up at our office with search warrants. Stew Jr. was in Arizona, preparing to give a speech at a corporate event. That morning, before the speech, he had called the office to check in, and that's when he heard the news. He finished his speech and caught the first flight home to help.

That night, I called a family meeting. Our entire family gathered around the dining room table at our house: Stew Jr., Tom, Beth, and Jill; their spouses; and Marianne and I. I broke the news about my building fund and that I had underreported my income to the IRS.

Stew and Tom offered to help me in any way they could. The first question was deciding how to respond to the media and all of our customers. I would be preoccupied with my defense attorneys and less involved in running our business than I'd been. Stew took on more responsibility in Norwalk and worked closely with Tom on the newly opened Danbury store.

The day after the IRS investigation started, the story hit the front pages of the local papers. Team Members came to work worried and confused. Rumors had sprung up at the store, and everyone wanted to know what was going on. Stew Jr. called a storewide meeting. He reassured everyone that the company was strong and that their jobs were secure. Stew demonstrated that he was the strong and secure leader that I knew he was. His leadership inspired the respect that everyone, especially his siblings, had for him.

Despite the news of the IRS investigation, our new store in Danbury had a successful grand opening. We had bridged a crucial test in our business—making the transition from one store to two—but the real test would come in the next couple of years. With the IRS investigation, the transition in management, and a recession, the early 1990s proved to be a very challenging time.

Another Bombshell Hits

The day in 1993 when I entered a guilty plea to the charges against me, Stew Jr., Tom, Beth, and Jill walked away from the New Haven federal courthouse with our business resting squarely on their shoulders. While Marianne and I had always intended to pass the company on to them, the IRS investigation escalated the whole process.

As much as the four were ready to run the company, because of the time they had already spent sharpening their skills, they were also four young, creative people with ideas and goals of their own. And there were still growing pains to be felt.

Probably the most difficult change was in Danbury. Opening the second store in Danbury had seemed like such a perfect answer: I had two capable sons but only one store. Now each would have their own store to run. But, the stores were part of the Stew Leonard's business structure, and only one person could run that. Until now, that had been me. Without me there, Stew Jr. was put in the difficult position of running the entire company, which included Tom's corner of the world in Danbury.

Although business in Danbury was growing faster than we had expected, Stew was under a lot of pressure to show our banks and suppliers that our business was solid and we would be able to pay any IRS fines and penalties. He needed a tight management structure.

At first, Tom understood that Stew was looking out for

the health of the whole business, but soon tension began to creep into their dealings with each other. Some of it was understandable. Tom had, after all, felt that he had built the Danbury store, transforming it from a seasonal produce tent to the most successful food store in town. It became successful under his watch. He felt he should be left alone to run it as he wanted. Stew Jr., on the other hand looked at the Danbury store as an extension of the business. Their relationship became difficult and Tom entered into the most difficult period of his life. He began drinking too much. The Danbury store had a hot dog cart out front and Tom was careless dealing with the cash.

Tom's behavior made a quiet impression on a few of his managers in Danbury, and eventually, the IRS opened an investigation into Tom's dealings. Tom regretted that he'd become so self-destructive, and he did several important things: he fully cooperated with the IRS, he left the company so as to not jeopardize the store's reputation further, and he joined Alcoholics Anonymous. At the hearing on the charges against him, Tom was sentenced to serve three and a half months in a halfway house.

I learned about Tom's conviction just after being transferred from McKean to Schuylkill Camp. I was walking around the track, trying to just get through one more day, when a friend came up to me and handed me his copy of *Forbes* magazine. Half laughing, he said, "Look, Stew, you made *Forbes*!"

I opened up the folded-over page and across the top of the

article was the headline "Like Father, Like Son." There was a big picture of Tom and a story about the hot dog cart. I went back to my little cinder-block cube and tried to come to grips with it. Obviously, it was all my fault—I'd let my family down: first, with my own stupid action and now with my son following my example. The shame of seeing that headline, that I'd brought all this upon my family, was hard enough to bear, and then I had to come to grips again with the fact that I was in prison. I felt alone and powerless.

But here again, sometimes from struggle comes strength. In a way, Tom's troubles turned out to have a silver lining for him. During his time at the halfway house, he was allowed to work. He called his friend Don Soderquist at Wal-mart and asked if they might have a job for him. Tom became a customer service consultant, traveling around to the stores within driving distance and helping them to identify and correct their customer service issues. After Tom was finished with his term at the halfway house, he took a job with Ukrops supermarkets in Richmond, Virginia. Merchandising has always been one of Tom's great strengths and within a year, he was offered an executive position with the famous British grocery giant ASDA. He was excited about moving his family to England and helping the British grocery chain refine its merchandising and marketing techniques. It was just the creative challenge he needed.

Stew Jr. Makes His Mark

If Tom was driven by his creative instincts, Stew was more logic-based and preferred a strategic style of management. He always looked for the professional thinking on a subject: how do the best companies do this? What is the standard in the industry? Then he would ask himself how can we do that and try to do it better? He sought out models to study, such as the weekly Saturday morning meetings that Wal-mart conducted, updating everyone from the chairman down to the checkers with current sales figures and other important information. He looked at how companies set strategic goals, communicated those goals to their employees, and achieved them; he studied production and efficiency structures; and he began implementing many of those elements in our company.

After I left for Minnesota, Stew stepped up these efforts. He knew that we needed financial credibility in order to maintain our good relationships with our suppliers and our banks. He had joined the Young Presidents Organization, an educational and networking group made up of presidents of successful companies. His YPO friends urged him to hire a heavyweight chief financial officer—someone who would bring world-class knowledge and expertise to the company. Then we would be poised not only for a stable future, but for growth. Stew brought in a search firm and was able to hire Vince Summa, who had been at Kraft General Foods.

The company was moving their headquarters from nearby Westchester County, and Vince didn't want to move his family. With Vince on board, Stew was better able to reassure our creditors that things were financially on solid footing.

By 1996, Stew's goal was to open a third store, and he had been looking for the right location. One day, one of his real estate agents called. He had just heard about what might be a perfect site: a forty- four-acre tract right on I-95 in Orange, Connecticut. Stew went up and took a look, and it was perfect indeed. The property sat at the junction of Interstate 95 and the main road into Orange. Stew was excited and was able to negotiate to buy the property. It seemed our third store would soon be on the way.

Stew quickly set the process in motion to get the permits we needed to begin building, but he ran into one roadblock after another. Several years later, the forty-four acres sat idle and we were still planning a store that seemed as if it might never materialize.

Then John Spencer, the mayor of Yonkers, New York, called. The fourth largest city in the state, Yonkers had faced deep financial troubles and was aggressively recruiting businesses that would bring jobs and tax revenue to the city. Mayor Spencer was a fan of ours and thought a Stew Leonard's food store would be a perfect fit. We had often received calls from other towns asking us to build a store, but this one was especially intriguing: the site was right off the New

York State Thruway, on the border of Westchester County and the Bronx—just 30 minutes from Times Square in Manhattan!

Spencer was very persistent and even drove up to Norwalk to personally discuss the incentives that Yonkers was willing to offer to encourage Stew Leonard's to come. When Stew walked the building site, he was impressed. The property sat at the top of a hill, with a view of the Empire State Building in the distance.

The building of the Yonkers store went smoothly, although Stew and his team had a lot to learn about operating in New York. The customers were different there; expectations were higher for some things and nonexistent for others. And the laws were different, too. But there was one huge difference that had tipped the scales right away: we were able to build a small wine shop at the corner of the Yonkers building. With the large number of "foodies" in the Westchester area, we were told, wine with the meal was an important factor. If we could sell wine, we would save our customers a trip to another shop. Stew and Kim had become wine aficionados, and Stew loved the idea of getting the family into the wine business.

But the wine shop was a risk. It was a new business altogether. Wine and spirits sales are highly regulated, and they are an expensive inventory investment. We knew the food business but knew little about the wine business.

Stew plunged all his efforts and all his best people into

It was a big honor when the city of Yonkers renamed the exit on the New York State Thruway Stew Leonard Drive!

building the Yonkers store and getting it up and running. Finally, all the plans and dreams that he'd had were coming true. The store opened to much fanfare. Customers loved the place, and the community—despite some early traffic-related problems —supported us. The wine shop was a home run. A few months after the store opened, Mayor Spencer called Stew. The turnpike exit that customers took from the thruway to Stew Leonard's, Costco, and Home Depot was called Corporate Drive, but there wasn't an office building in sight. He asked how his father would like seeing the name changed to Stew Leonard Drive.

A few months later, Stew and I drove down to Yonkers. He had something to show me, he said. As we passed through the tollbooth, Stew slowed down and pointed. I looked up, and there a huge green-and-white sign proclaimed the exit as Stew Leonard Drive. I couldn't believe my eyes!

Finding a Place in the Fortune Top 100

While Stew was tending to the big picture of opening new stores and helming the growth of the company, Jill and Beth were handling many of the day-to-day issues. Jill was flourishing in human resources with Karen Mazako. It was right where she had always wanted to be. She loved working with the staff and seeing our Team Members grow both as people and as professionals. As Jill's management skills became stronger, her job became not only to hire and train, but also to manage communications such as our bimonthly newsletter, *Stew's News*, and our daily newsletter for Team Members, which let everyone know not only what was going on in each of our stores, but also with each other. She also became involved in many of our charity events, from broad-ranging fundraisers to Team Members' favorite charities, such as breast cancer and multiple sclerosis walks. Her job had become anything and everything that concerned our Team Members and their jobs.

One day Stew Jr. walked into Jill's office with a copy of *Fortune* magazine in his hand.

"Look at this," he said, pointing to the "Best 100 Companies to Work For In America" list that the magazine had just published. The companies were lauded for their platinum-quality health plans (which we had), for their extensive training (which we did), for their high-quality customer service (check!), and for the career opportunities they offered their employees (something we prided ourselves on).

"I wonder if we could possibly make this list," Stew asked.

Jill looked closely at the list of companies, and she realized that for practically every reason that companies were chosen for the list, she could come up with similar things that we were also doing that might help us win a spot. Submitting our name for consideration the next year became Jill's project.

Jill and Karen began the application process and submitted the necessary documents for consideration, and then they waited. The following January, in 2002, the *Fortune* list was published, and everyone at Stew Leonard's was elated: we were ranked number 22.

Jill applied again the next year, and the next, and the next. But it wasn't just a matter of filling out a form and sending in some articles. With each application, Jill looked for things we could do that could make our company an even better place to work. We cut Team Members' health care premium

Top: Jill and Karen Mazako beamed with pride when we landed at number 22 on Fortune's *"100 Best Companies to Work For In America in 2002."*

Bottom: To celebrate this honor we threw a big party for our entire team.

contribution to zero; we added in-house health care diagnostic clinics; we held more free lunches, parties, and Team Member outings; we added new training and promotion opportunities; and we increased our charitable contributions and our Team Member profit sharing—whatever we could do to make our Team's experience the best it could be. Jill highlighted these items in each application, and her hard work has been rewarded. Although the number of companies applying to be on the list practically doubles each year, Jill and Karen's efforts put Stew Leonard's on the list for eight years in a row.

Beth's Creativity Carves a Unique Path

Food retailing and baking was in Beth's blood, and once she married, it was on both sides of her family. Beth's husband, Bill, whose father had a popcorn business, worked for General Foods. But eventually we convinced him to come to work at Stew Leonard's. He started off in Norwalk by bringing his popcorn recipes and coffee-roasting expertise to the company. Then he joined Tom and Danny at our Danbury store. When Beth became pregnant with Sarah, she decided she wanted to stay home until her children started school full-time, and Bill took over the Bethy's Bakery operations as well. He soon was in charge of our entire fresh food merchandising, overseeing our kitchen and deli and hot food operations as well.

A few years later, when Sarah went off to kindergarten, Beth was ready to return to the store. Bill had left the company to open his own bakery. Beth noticed that more and more customers were asking us to ship our products to their friends and family as gifts, so she and Steve Guthman created a mail-order catalogue. Soon she was shipping her award-winning brownies and chocolate chip cookies in Stew Leonard's tins, along with picnic baskets, snack baskets, get-well baskets and holiday baskets.

Customers loved being able to send things from their favorite store to friends, and companies began sending our baskets as corporate gifts. Before we knew it, Beth had set up a catalogue on our Web site. Now her gift department fills more than 100,000 orders every year.

A Dream of Tom's Own

Tom loved working in London, but his wife Karen missed her family in Richmond. A year after they moved to London, Karen's mother had a stroke, and Karen felt she needed to care for her. During the first few months back in Virginia, Tom became restless. He had loved the experience of building and opening the Danbury store, and one day he called me to float his newest idea: opening his own store in Richmond.

I loved the idea. It would put Tom on a path that he would find fulfilling; he never had been as happy working for someone else as he'd been being his own boss. If we could just find the ideal site for Tom's new store, it would be the perfect solution for us all.

Marianne and I flew to Richmond to help Tom search for the right site. Tom and I drove around the city during the first week. Rather than look for a high-priced main road location, we scoured the town looking for what I called a "backyard location." In other words, a lower priced site that was just off of a main artery where it would be convenient for regular customers to come back over and over on their way doing other errands. Finally, we found it. It was just off Interstate 64, in an area called Short Pump. Because there was already one of the finest food merchandisers in the country nearby, Ukrops, and a Wal-Mart and Kroger within a mile, competition would be very tough. But for miles and miles in every direction, there were brand-new subdivisions filled with brand-new houses with lots of little children. These would provide customers galore! I spotted a sign just behind a BestBuy store. The sign advertised six acres for sale, a level span of woods and fields that was a straight shot to West Broad Street, the main thoroughfare. It was the perfect site for Tom's new 10,000-square-foot store: Tom Leonard's Farmer's Market.

With his emphasis on fresh-from-the-farm quality at low down-on-the-farm prices, Tom Leonard's Farmer's Market quickly was on the top of the local media "best" lists: "the

Tom took his marketing ideas to Virginia and opened Tom Leonard's Farmer's Market in Richmond in 2004.

Best of Richmond," "the Best Place to Take Kids," "the Best Local Produce," "50 Fantastic Food Finds," and on and on. In return, Tom delighted his customers by planning lots of fun activities in his store, from movie nights to Halloween-costume contests to hayrides and pumpkin patches—all of course, with costumed characters and dancing, singing animatronics. Somewhere he had learned the importance of making your customers say WOW!

Visiting Richmond and seeing Tom's store always reminds me of the early days of Stew Leonard's nearly forty years earlier. I smile seeing Tom with his sleeves rolled up, arrang-

Buying directly from the farmer assures top quality for our customers. Stew and Tom show off fresh-picked berries on the farm in California.

ing tomato displays or piling up fresh corn, or handing out freshly baked chocolate cookies to the kids. Not a day goes by that he isn't living the old adage: "The farmer's shadow is the best fertilizer." It's a thrill to see some of the philosophies I've always believed put to work at Tom's store: his large carved wooden sign, for example, thanking his customers, showing his gratitude for their loyalty, says "Welcome! We're Glad You Came!" Tom even has a huge rock at his front door chiseled with his customer service policy:

Rule 1 The customer is always right!

Rule 2 If the customer is ever wrong, reread Rule 1.

Tom has always been full of fresh ideas and energy, and now he has a chance to display it in his own store. But the best, by far, is seeing the excitement and happiness of the hundreds of customers leaving the store with full shopping carts and big smiles on their faces.

chapter nine

GROOMING THE NEXT GENERATION

The years passed quickly and before we knew it, it was 2002 and time to celebrate our fiftieth wedding anniversary. When Marianne and I were married in 1952, we had a small, intimate wedding. Our families did everything they could to make the occasion meaningful and festive. As a wedding present, Marianne's mom gave us her prized collection of hand-painted dishes that had once belonged to the German royal family. They were heirlooms that she had purchased many years earlier at an estate auction in Germany. We were able to use them for our wedding reception. My mother made Marianne's wedding dress as well as all of the bridesmaids' dresses. After the ceremony at St. Mary's Church on West Avenue in Norwalk, our families and friends gathered on the sun porch of the home on Partrick Avenue where I grew up. It was a joyous and memorable day.

Our one big extravagance was a honeymoon to Bermuda. It had always sounded like such a magical place to us and we dreamed of bicycling around its countryside dressed in Bermuda shorts, just like we had seen in the advertisements for the island.

We were delighted when Stew Jr., Tom, Beth, and Jill got together and suggested a return visit to Bermuda. But we were even more thrilled when they told us that they and all of their kids would come, too, and that they had arranged for Marianne and me to have a wedding ceremony to renew our vows.

Marianne and I leave St. Mary's Church on our wedding day in 1952.

Fifty years after our wedding we returned to Bermuda with our entire family—four children, their four spouses, and thirteen grandchildren—to renew our vows and conduct our first family business conference.

It would be the vacation of a lifetime, and we certainly had a lot to celebrate besides fifty years together. My IRS experience was behind me; all of my fines, penalties, and taxes had been paid in full. All community service work had been completed and the whole affair was now entirely behind us, and our business was growing nicely. Stew Jr., Beth, and Jill were all making their marks at Stew Leonard's, and Tom was busy building his own store. We began to plan for the first complete gathering of the Leonard family, all twenty-three of us.

Since we would all be together, it would be the ideal time to have not only a family reunion, but also our first "Family Business Retreat." It would be a meeting in which we could begin to lay the foundations for the third generation to join the family business that someday would be theirs.

It was very important to Marianne and me that our grandchildren understand the family legacy and appreciate the business as something precious to be preserved. Not only had it taken two generations to create, it was the fulfillment of our dreams. But as family businesses move into the third generation, things can get sticky. Some of the grandchildren may choose separate paths; some may find Stew Leonard's to be a good place to work; but others may develop a passion to do something on their own.

While Marianne and I were lucky in that our own four children chose careers with the company, when they were growing up we emphasized that we wanted each of them to choose a career that they wanted. But we also taught them that they could each find a passion somewhere within the family business, just as I had done. And each one did eventually find a place in the business they aspired to, and when the baton was passed to them, they were ready to run with it. Our grandchildren will be offered that same baton, and we want them to be able to see the value in the opportunity, to see the roles they might play, and to be ready to run with that baton. But if they choose a different career, we want them to pursue it. I have always told our children what my dad had told me: "You can become anything you want in this world providing you want it bad enough, are willing to pay the price, and stick to it long enough."

It is a sad fact that 95 percent of all family businesses fail within ten years. In fact, surveys show that only 15 percent survive past the second generation. If the marketplace doesn't get them, family rivalry does. The few that do survive face a unique set of problems: a board of directors made up of family members who may not have any interest in being involved in the business; family members who have not earned their titles; a company leadership that is dictated by a committee rather than a leader; and heirs who just want as much cash as possible from their inheritance and then to just live happily ever after. The last thing that Marianne and I want our grandkids to have to go through is the squabbling that is all too common in many second- and third-generation family businesses. Many countries in the world have a saying that illustrates this: "Shirtsleeves to shirtsleeves in three generations."

Dr. Danco was never shy about telling us the challenges of raising children to take over a family business. First, there's the question of imparting values to the second generation, or G2 as we call it. Successful entrepreneurs work long, hard days and carefully attend to every detail to build their businesses, and because of that, they develop a strong work ethic. But the children and grandchildren usually don't have to work as hard as the founders did, so very often their values aren't as strong or even the same.

Then there's the issue of advantages: once entrepreneurs achieve financial success, they often take great pleasure in showering their children with luxuries (of course they want to give their kids the things they themselves didn't have), and the kids sometimes grow up taking it all for granted and developing a different set of values.

All of this can be even more exaggerated with the third generation, G3, which very often doesn't share the same drive and commitment that the entrepreneur needed to build the business from scratch. Dr. Danco made us realize early on that we would have to work very hard to make sure that our children and grandchildren are aware of these issues.

Another reason that some family businesses don't make a successful transition from one generation to the next is that the founders remain in the top job way past the time when they should retire. They hate to let go. They feel that they are indispensible. They don't feel that the next generation is capable of running things without them. This is an extremely common problem. My stupid building fund had forced our second generation to step up to the plate and run the company while I was away for forty-two months. Fortunately, they had been prepared and were ready to accept the challenge.

Although I had promoted Stew Jr. to president, Tom, Beth, and Jill, his vice presidents, had their own opinions on issues that faced the business. These were things that they would have normally come to me with. Luckily, I was able to continue to communicate with them even though the burden rested fully on their shoulders to work things out.

Marianne and I have always known that all thirteen grandkids would probably not want to work in the business. But the grandkids, whether they choose a career with us or not, would always have a place in running the company. To prepare them for this, we drew up a Leonard Family Plan. We structured the framework for our family council and began work on the Leonard Family Handbook. We made a plan to share all of this information with the grandchildren at regular intervals, so that there would be no big surprises down the road.

Our three main goals were to build a philosophical foundation for the company that is so solid that it can't be undermined; to anticipate the problems and challenges that will come up; and to do everything we can to grow our grandchildren into the leaders the company will need to make it to the fourth generation.

Families That Play Together Stay Together

With the groundwork in place, the timing of our wedding anniversary trip to Bermuda couldn't have been better. We used the time to increase the camaraderie and to conduct informal discussion meetings. Several of the grandkids were still young and needed supervision, so we were able to build trust and respect by having the older cousins watch the younger ones, whether it was babysitting while the adults went to dinner or taking them on a horseback ride. Best of all, the children all loved being together, because some of their very best friends were right there in their own family. So most important, they all had fun together.

Our morning work sessions were casual and relaxed. There were lots of question-and-answer sessions that included conversations about our three stores: Norwalk, Danbury and Yonkers. We talked about the future; we asked for the older grandkids' input. Should we open a fourth store? What impact will Tom's store, which was about to open in Virginia, have on the family business? We talked about the challenges we had faced and the philosophy that had not only helped us earn our successes, but also helped us through the difficult times as well.

Stew, Tom, Beth, and Jill had come to Bermuda excited and enthusiastic about teaching their children what it truly means to be a part of our growing family business. Discussions were lively and fun, and all the exuberance of our business was part of every meeting, every dinner, every outing that we had that week. When we returned, we all came back as members of a much more enlightened Leonard family.

In fact, the week was such a success that as soon as we got home, we decided that every few years all twenty-three of us would spend a week focused on building up the next generation of family leadership. We asked the grandchildren for their input on where we should go to for our next retreat. The choice was unanimous: our second retreat took place three years later at Disney World in the spring of 2005. From then on, it was every two years.

A Family That "Sticks" Together

During the second family business conference, we focused on the history of our business. We had collected family pictures going back to the days of my grandfather, pictures of my parents, the horse and wagon that my father used to deliver milk, of Clover Farms Dairy, and of the early days of Stew Leonard's. We put together everything in a Leonard history slide show. I acted as moderator, explaining the challenges of building the Norwalk store, and the philosophies behind what Stew Leonard's is today. The grandchildren had heard the eggnog story several times, and they had been able to recite Rule 1 and Rule 2 since they were toddlers, but I explained them again to emphasize the ideals that are the foundation of our business.

First, I stressed the fact that "families that play together stay together." With all of the adversities our business has faced and those we've endured personally, it was family sticking together that made the difference between success and failure.

To demonstrate the strength of family, I dramatized the point with a little lesson right out of one of Aesop's Fables. I handed out a ten-inch-long pencil-size stick to each person in the room. Then I asked everyone at the count of three, to try to break their sticks in half. They all took great glee in successfully snapping their sticks in half.

Then I announced, "Now I'm going to pass this bundle of twenty-three identical sticks around the room. The only difference is that I have taped the twenty-three sticks together so they are one unit. I'd like each of you to try to break the bundle of sticks in half. Please keep passing it to the person next to you and let's see if anyone can."

Each person took a try, but no one was able to break the bundle in half. And then I made my point: "As a family, as long as we all stick together, no one can break us either. We are much stronger by sticking together.

"It was this strength of our family all sticking together that got us through our most trying times," I said, and then, as unpleasant as it was, I explained to them all about my building fund and why I had been sent to a federal prison camp for underreporting my income.

"That experience taught me a lot of things. Most important, it taught me how much I love everybody in this room. Without my family, camp would have been ten times more difficult for me.

"While I was away, we had problems with the business," I told the grandchildren. "Some of them almost seemed insurmountable, but your parents all rose to the occasion and did a marvelous job of handling them." It was then, I told them, that I realized exactly how effective a leader Stew Jr.

had become, and that my role would no longer be that of quarterback, but that I would now become the coach on the sidelines and Stew would be the quarterback.

"I will still be here for any help that any of you might ask of me," I told the grandchildren. "But my main goal is going to become your number one cheerleader."

Then I shared with them the words of the great Roman poet Horace, who said, "*Carpe diem quam minimum credula postero*," which means, "Seize the day, trust little to tomorrow." The point is that yesterday is over and done with. Tomorrow may never come; today is all there is. It's something we believe in so strongly that we named our vacation home in St. Martin Carpe Diem.

"I asked my mom one day, when she was ninety-three, if she had any regrets. She said 'No, Stewart, when you get to my age and look back on your life, you don't so much regret the things that didn't turn out the way you wanted them to. No, instead, you regret the things that you were going to do but just never got around to doing.'

"So when you see something that you dream of doing, do it," I told them.

We planned our third family business conference for the summer of 2007. We decided to take everyone on a Mediterranean cruise that stopped in towns along the coast of Italy. We would have our meetings each morning in one of the ship's conference rooms. TJ, Blake, Emma, Jennie Lynne, Sarah, and Jake were all in college, and the rest of the grandkids were in high school or middle school. Most of them were at the point that they were beginning to think seriously about what they would need to do to prepare for a career.

That summer we also unveiled the Leonard Family Handbook. This was the set of guidelines that Stew Jr., Tom, Beth, and Jill had created. Among other things, it would help the grandchildren learn about careers at Stew Leonard's. We had never had formal rules for working at the store; in the early days, our children worked where they were needed. As adults, each found a place in the company, worked hard, and earned the respect of their co-workers. But now that we were a bigger company, with more than 2,000 Team Members, a formal process was necessary.

To prepare our grandchildren for the future of either working for Stew Leonard's or holding a position on the advisory board, each one is encouraged to work at the store during school holidays and summer vacations. Their first jobs have to be on the front lines, working alongside other Team Members in a job that involves customer contact. They earn the going rate for the job plus 10 percent (a family-member bonus.) They receive no special perks or privileges. We feel that developing good work habits is one of the real secrets to success, and that happiness comes from the successful achievement of goals.

As a result of these family guidelines, all of the grandchildren have worked during their summer vacations bagging groceries and ringing up customers; shucking corn in produce, cutting up salmon in the fish department; slicing ham

Our grandchildren enjoy working at our stores during school vacations (left to right, top row: Jake, Rex, Andrew, Will; bottom row: Madison, Britt, Chase, Ryann, Sarah).

in the deli; roasting coffee; working in the catering department; baking cookies; stocking the milk coolers; serving ice cream cones; and taking complaints in the customer service department. They've contributed to our company newsletter, *Stew's News* and to our publicity campaigns, and they've had a hand in hiring and training in the human resources department. They've all gotten invaluable experience by working side by side with other Team Members.

And they are contributing a lot, too. One summer, Stew's daughter Chase was working in the bakery when she came up with a suggestion: to package and sell our cookie dough. We put a cooler right there between the bakery racks with freshly made dough that customers could take home so they could bake their own cookies. Jill's daughter Britt found a brand of bottled ice tea that she really liked and championed it through the buying and merchandising process. It became one of our best sellers. Will and Andrew, Beth's sons, and Jill's son Jake created their own new product in our Norwalk store. One day while working in the juice department, they mistakenly added grapefruit juice to a vat of fresh orange juice. Next we knew, they were sampling their new product, half grapefruit and half orange juice, which they christened "Fusion." It's tangy, refreshing, and always fresh-squeezed; today it's one of our most popular products.

Learning the Nuts and Bolts of Dairy and Produce

One day when Jake was working in the coffee department and I had stopped by to see him, Andrew, the store's president, came by with a new product he was thinking of purchasing for the holiday season, a red fire truck that children could sit in and pedal. Andrew hadn't had time to show it to any customers yet. He said to Jake, "How about asking 100 customers if they would buy this fire truck and how much they would be willing to pay? Let's find out what they think about the idea of us selling it."

Jake, who was only fifteen at the time, wasn't crazy about the idea of standing at the front of the store with a red fire truck, asking strangers questions, did just that. That day, Jake realized that customers don't bite. They were happy to be asked for their input. He even presented the results of his survey at the next manager's meeting, and everyone agreed with him that based on our customer reactions, it wouldn't be a good idea to sell the fire truck.

Another rule that we have is requiring our grandchildren to work for another company after college. At first I didn't feel it was necessary, but we soon realized that it would help them bring another perspective and real-world experience to their jobs at Stew Leonard's.

And the grandkids have embraced this rule. Blake, the first to graduate, interned at Rachael Ray's television show in New York one summer during college, and her first job out of college was with an Italian winery in Tuscany. She is presently working for the Gallo wine family in California. Sarah spent a summer interning with a New York City catering company. I now am convinced that such experiences with other companies will be great for all of the grandchildren.

But as much as we'd like all of the grandchildren to build their careers at Stew Leonard's, it's not going to happen. During our trip to Europe, Tom's son TJ sat down with his father, Stew Jr., and me to explain how he felt about a career in the food business. He said that after spending his weekends in high school working for his father at Tom Leonard's Farmers Market in Richmond, and previously having worked at Stew Leonard's in Norwalk, he had come to the conclusion that it just wasn't for him; his heart wasn't in food retailing. Where his heart really did soar was in the cockpit of his father's little

Mooney airplane. He had been flying with his dad as his "co-pilot" since he was a little boy and Tom was running our Danbury store. What he dreamed of was becoming a professional pilot. His father, Stew Jr., and I quickly responded, "No problem!" I've always told my own four children that the most important thing was for them to be happy and fulfilled. That fall, TJ left for the Parks College flight school at the University of St. Louis in Missouri.

During our Mediterranean family business conference, we were all invited to get an up-close look at another very famous family business: Antinori Vineyards. While learning his way around the wine business, Stew had become friends with Allegra Antinori. Allegra, who represents the twenty-sixth generation of the family business, invited our entire family to be her guests at the family estate, Castella della Sala, a magnificent winery and vineyard near Livorno, halfway between Rome and Florence. We arranged for a bus to take us to Tuscany for the day. Not only was it a great chance for our grandkids to hear the story of another family business, but the day also gave us insight into our newest growth business: wine. As Allegra gave us a tour of the vineyards and winery, she told us the story of how their business has endured for so many generations. We all loved learning about the wine-making process, the cellars, and the vineyards. The beautiful summer day was topped off with a luncheon served out on the estate's lawn, and Allegra shared with us what it was like to be a member of possibly one of the oldest family businesses on earth. Our day in Tuscany turned out to be the highlight of our Italy trip.

Opportunities for Advancement

By 2006, it had been ten years since we had purchased the land in Orange, Connecticut, and begun to apply for our building and zoning permits. We had hit roadblock after roadblock. A single group of Orange residents appealed every approval we won, stalling our progress. But believing that we would someday be building

The happy family at work together at their family business. Beth is next to me, then Jill, Marianne, Stew Jr., and Tom.

our next store, we continued preparing for growth inside the company. Our human resources department was training and promoting managers and assistant managers so that we would always have them ready to transfer to a new store once it was built.

Stew believes that we have an obligation to our Team Members to grow the company; they worked hard and made the company better by learning and growing professionally. He believes that we owe it to them to provide opportunities for advancement.

One day, Stew received a call from Rodney Mortensen, the mayor of Newington, Connecticut, a suburban town just south of Hartford. Would we consider building a store there?

Since we'd opened the Yonkers store and received publicity for being on *Fortune's* list of the "100 Best Companies to Work For in America," we'd gotten even more calls from officials who wanted us to open in their town. Stew would always politely decline.

But when Mayor Mortensen called, he explained that there was a former Caldor store there that had been sitting empty for a number of years. Newington was in the process of trying to revitalize its retail corridor, the Berlin Turnpike. The town felt that a Stew Leonard's would do well there.

Previously, we had always believed that we needed to own the land that our stores sat on, but leasing space had worked out well in Yonkers. Stew went up and looked at the site, then signed a lease and got to work planning our fourth store.

Stew quickly put together his team to manage the building and opening of the new store. Luckily, we had the perfect person ready and waiting to run the Newington store, my nephew Dan Arthur, who had been groomed for the opportunity since he was a teenager. Stew, Dan, and the team analyzed every detail about the Norwalk, Danbury, and Yonkers stores that worked, and they especially looked at those systems that they felt might be improved. They considered everything from the merchandise mix to market demographics. They looked at how to better locate workstations, refrigeration, and loading docks. They analyzed customer flow, department locations, and where to build an in-store dining area. They studied everything from the types of materials used for flooring to the kind of hand dryers we had in the restrooms. And they looked for ways they could improve all of it.

The benefit of opening a store at the invitation of the mayor, as we had found out in Yonkers, was that the building process goes much faster. The town of Newington helped by guiding us through the permits process and smoothing the way past some of the problems that popped up. Just one year after we had agreed to open there, the former Caldor "box store" was transformed into the dairy barn that our customers know so well, with its custom-designed displays and departments, the center-aisle "labyrinth" that guides shoppers past every department, more animatronics than in any of our other stores, and a large wine shop. While we promoted quite a few people from our other stores into management positions in Newington, we still had to hire a few hundred local Team Members, most of whom trained in the store and helped to get their departments ready for the grand opening.

On the eve of opening day in April 2007, we threw a big party in the Newington store, complete with food from our kitchens, wine from our wine distributors, and music and dancing. Stew Jr. hired the famous entertainer Chubby Checker to perform on a stage set up inside the store. There were photographers and local TV news crews taking pictures and taping stories, and there were TV interviews with Mayor Mortensen and Connecticut Governor Jodi Rell. But the most exciting part of the whole evening for me was the dozens and dozens of new Team Members who came up to say how happy they were to be a part of Stew Leonard's. The next morning, the store opened to rave reviews from customers and the local media, including the *Hartford Courant.*

The Newington wine shop was also received with cheers. With five successful wine stores, Stew began to look at the wine business as something that perhaps we could expand in addition to the food stores, rather than as an extension of them. The time might be right to build freestanding wine stores. With that plan, Stew and his wine team decided to tackle one of the largest retail communities in the country: New Jersey.

But in New Jersey, not only is the land expensive and the retail landscape dense, it is extremely difficult to apply for and receive a liquor license. As luck would have it, Stew found a wine store in Clifton and another one in Paramus that had liquor licenses and whose owners had decided to sell. Suddenly, we opened two new wine shops in New Jersey. They, too, were well received and within only a few months were doing the volume that we had hoped for. But the most surprising thing about our new freestanding wine shops was the question that we got the most: When are you going to open the food store next to it?

chapter ten

THE BOTTOM LINE

One day, the phone rang. It was my friend Woody Woodruff, the former general manager of the *Bradford Era* newspaper. The Bradford Merchants' Workshop members wanted Marianne and me to come to Bradford for a dinner in my honor. On the one hand, I was very honored and moved by the fact that they felt that I had made such a difference in their lives that they wanted to formally thank me. On the other hand, I wasn't sure I really wanted to revisit and relive the unpleasant memories of the time I spent incarcerated at McKean. My first reaction was to say, "Thank you but no thank you." I didn't think I wanted to go back to Bradford.

But Marianne had a different opinion.

"Stew, think of all your friends, the merchants in town," she said. "Think of how nice it would be to see the changes they have made. Think of how you'd be able to actually see how they put some of your advice to work. Don't forget, while you may have helped them, they also helped you."

The more I thought about my old friends in Bradford and how working with the merchants association had helped me get through my experience, the more I realized that Marianne was right. Once again, her good sense changed my mind, and I decided to accept their extremely kind invitation.

Our son Tom, as he had so many times while I was at McKean, piloted the flight to Bradford, but for the first time I was with him and Marianne as a passenger. We checked into the Fisher Inn, which was owned by Brenda Ruth, whom I'd gotten to know as a part of the merchants' workshop. Brenda was happy to see us, and she shared many of the good things that had happened to her and her business. She also told us of many of the happenings in Bradford, the businesses that had closed, the ones that had changed hands, and the ones that were new.

Brenda said that the whole town was buzzing about what she called the "Stew Leonard Day" party that would be held that night. Her excitement instantly made me forget the reason I was sent to Bradford in the first place and put me right back with my friends at the merchants' workshop. It was amazing: rather than reflecting on the difficult times at McKean, I could only think of the happy, positive times with all my old friends. It felt great.

Marianne and I spent the afternoon with Woody Woodruff and Reverend Bob Brest. We had lunch at Chu Lee Garden and visited with Betty Chu, who had been part of the workshop. Then we walked around the town, going into many of the stores and visiting with the owners. I saw so many things that day that I had heard about but had never seen. It was rewarding to finally see all their businesses, their stores, their employees, and their customers.

As we walked by one of the storefronts, I was surprised to see that Grant Orris's jewelry store had closed, and I asked Woody what had happened. Woody reminded me of a story from one of our workshop sessions.

I had stressed the importance of customer service and of having the same customers come back over and over. Grant Orris told us about a young couple who came into his store and asked if he would clean their high school class rings. "I remembered what we talked about the week before and I took both of their rings and put them into my ultrasonic cleaning machine.

"While we were waiting, the young couple told me how they had just been to my competitor's large jewelry store around the corner and how they had refused to clean their rings because they said that they were 'too busy.'" After Grant had the rings sparkling clean, he rubbed them with his polishing cloth and told the young couple that there would be no charge, and thanked them for coming in.

Grant went on, "Then I forgot all about it until later that

same year, the young couple became engaged. And where do you think they purchased their $5,000 engagement ring?"

Then Woody broke into a huge smile and pointed around the corner.

"Grant has moved his jewelry store to the space where that competing jewelry store had been."

You Can Go Home Again!

That night we gathered in the conference room of the Best Western Hotel in downtown Bradford. Woody had arranged to have the party catered, he'd set up a bar, and more than a hundred people came! The room was packed with all the merchants I'd worked with, as well as former Warden Dennis Luther. There were even a few who were new since I'd been there. Many of them hadn't seen each other in a while. After Luther retired, the new warden had discontinued the merchants' workshops, and the members no longer met as a group. That night was like a class reunion, everyone was glad to see each other, catching up and getting reacquainted.

Finally Woody went up to the front of the room to introduce me. He was overflowing with enthusiasm.

"The *Guinness Book of World Records* has spotlighted our speaker's store as having sales per square foot greater than any other single food store in the world. Ripley's Believe It or Not has featured his business as the world's largest dairy store. Each week more than 100,000 customers shop there.

To put that figure into perspective, that is the same number of people the Rose Bowl holds."

The lights dimmed, and a picture flashed up on the big screen. It was a photograph of the Rose Bowl, packed with a crowd watching a football game.

"Tom Peters, author of the best-selling book *In Search of Excellence* said, and I quote, 'I've searched the world over looking for excellence in every nook and cranny. One of the best examples I've found is a single dairy store in Norwalk, Connecticut.' The fellow who created that store is with us today. He started out as a milkman, and one day found himself at the White House receiving the Presidential Award for Entrepreneurial Excellence from the president of the United States, Ronald Reagan. Please help me welcome our friend, Stew Leonard!"

Everybody stood up and started clapping. Standing there looking at the faces of all of my hardworking friends, I got a little choked up. I began by telling everyone how sincerely honored I felt to be there. It was a heartfelt experience and I thanked them for the support they gave me while I was incarcerated and for inviting me up to Bradford. But most important of all, I told them that I was very proud of all they had done to improve their town.

Then I showed a slide of our big fifty-foot-high electronic road sign in front of our Norwalk store.

"This sign usually advertises our specials, like this." The sign in the photograph read "MILK $.69 ½ Gal."

Then another picture popped up on the screen, showing

the sign with another message: "WE LOVE BRADFORD MERCHANTS!"

I was so honored that the Bradford merchants asked me to return for a reunion that I put a message up in lights on our electric road sign at the Norwalk store.

The audience applauded. Then I said, "Please don't get carried away, because if you had driven by one minute after the picture was taken, you would have seen the sign flashing this message again: "MILK $.69 ½ Gal""

The audience roared with laughter.

Tonight I'd like to tell everyone what a privilege it was working with such a great group during our Bradford Merchants' Workshop days. Your enthusiasm at each week's class was something that inspired me from week to week. I want to thank you all for your friendship as well as your contributions. I appreciate all of you very much.

"In preparing for tonight, I thought about a few basic ideas that we all must continually remember as merchants. I'd like to share with you tonight those things that are working for me today in my business and I think will work for you, too.

"As we all know, most of the good ideas in any business often originate with the customers. Just last week I had one suggest that we sell little Beanie Baby dolls. I said, 'Sell dolls in a food store? I never thought of that.' But I decided to try it anyway and soon brought in the full line of Beanie Babies dolls. We immediately were amazed at the way the customers and the children flocked to the display. Once again, that's an example of how important it is to listen to your customers and keep an open mind.

"Next, it's important to realize that you as the manager or owner are extremely important to your business. Every business is really just an extension of the person in charge. Just as the melting snow on the top of the mountain trickles down the entire mountain, so too does the business owner's enthusiasm and personality trickle down through the entire organization. At any business you enter, you can practically feel the presence of the owner. Unfortunately, when the owner is not present, you can feel that, too. The truth is, every person's business is a portrait of himself or herself.

"Of course, we can't run our businesses alone. We need good people to help us. At Stew's, most of our management people were promoted from within. We found that we are way better off growing our own people for our management jobs. We feel that loyalty is more valuable than operational skills. We can always teach skills, but loyalty is something you can't teach.

"Our hiring principles are simple: Hire the smile! As my daughter Jill says, 'We don't train people to be nice, we hire nice people to train!' It's almost impossible to change people's attitude. Therefore, it's critically important that we surround ourselves with happy, positive people—people who work with us, not against us. One of the best ways to grow your people is to become more of a coach and teacher and less of a do-it-yourself type.

"Next, remember that perception is everything. Last Sunday, when I drove into my store's parking lot at 6:00 a.m. I noticed that there were papers and cups from some of the local fast food places scattered along the edge of our flower beds. They'd been dropped there on Saturday night. It would have only taken me a few minutes to pick them up myself, but instead I got our store manager, Roy Snider, and we both spent thirty minutes walking around the parking lot discussing the importance of perception. I wasn't interested in having a clean parking lot for just that one day. My goal was to keep it clean the next week, and the week after that. I tried to emphasize how important it was for Roy to look at our business through the customers' eyes. A dirty parking lot might indicate that things inside the store might be dirty, too. That's why we bend over backward to keep our restrooms spotless, and there's always a vase of fresh flowers on the counters.

"Perception is very important. My daughter Beth started our Bethy's Bakery by baking homemade chocolate chip cookies and giving the warm cookies out as samples. She makes all of her products from scratch. The point is that you can grow any business if you continually pay attention to the details. But you cannot forget the importance of perception. For example, last week a customer mentioned to Beth that the Arthur Avenue Bakery in the Bronx had wonderful hard rolls, so even though Beth bakes her own hard rolls, she went and bought a few cases from the Arthur Avenue Bakery to see how our customers liked them before changing her own recipe. On Monday, a friend, Cheri Batson, and her mother and father visited us from St. Martin, where she has a restaurant.

"As I was giving her a tour of our store, Cheri said, 'Stew, I didn't realize that you bought most of your products from other bakeries.' I assured her that Beth baked everything from scratch. She said, 'But Stew, look at those cases of rolls with Arthur Avenue Bakery written on the box!'

"Her perception was that since Arthur Avenue was written on the boxes of rolls, that everything else was bought from other bakeries, too. So take a close look at your business and imagine what your customer's perception is.

"I hope you will all have a chance to meet my son Tom tonight. Tom has just returned from England, where he consulted with the giant supermarket chain ASDA. You may have read about ASDA. It was just bought by Wal-mart for more than $10.8 billion.

"Tom initiated a special project for them. He used the Pareto principle, also known as the 80/20 rule, which we discussed during our workshop meetings. Tom saved ASDA money by eliminating many of the items that were not contributing much to their total sales. But the real payoff was that besides simplifying their stores and warehouses, Tom filled the extra space on the shelves with their fastest-moving items. Enlarging their displays of their most popular items meant sales increased. Shopping became simpler. Customers loved it. You can use the very same principle in your stores.

"Most of the large national chain supermarkets are going in the opposite direction. I recently talked with my friend Bob Tobin, who was chairman of Stop & Shop supermarkets. He explained that a typical new Super Stop & Shop Supermarket stocks more than 80,000 items. At Stew's, we sell fewer than 2,000 items! That's less than 3 percent of what the chain stores sell. Yet our sales are larger. It's not the number of items you sell that is important, it's whether the items are the products that your customers need and want to buy.

"You can do the same thing in your business. Remember: winners focus, losers spray. The more you simplify your product line, the more you'll sell. It may sound crazy, but it works.

"The final point I'd like to stress tonight is the importance of making your customers say WOW! I wish I could take you all on a magic carpet ride to visit our store in Connecticut. But since that's not possible, I've put together some slides of how we try to make our customers say WOW!"

I showed them slides of our dancing animatronics, with little children standing wide-eyed, watching the banjo-playing cows; Wow the Cow and Daphne Duck, our costumed characters, greeting people in our store's aisles; Team Members dressed in Halloween costumes; Stew Jr. giving an oversized check to the local United Way; lines of customers waiting for lobster dinners; and smiling customers leaving our store, their carts practically overflowing with Stew Leonard's bags.

The audience stood and applauded, and practically the entire room came up to the front to shake hands and speak with me. But I was the one doing the thanking. It was great to see everyone in Bradford again. Despite my initial reservations, I was back with my friends. That visit to Bradford did far more for me than it did for them.

We're Bonkers for Yonkers!

The next day, Marianne, Tom, and I returned home to Connecticut, where the company was buzzing with excitement over our next venture: the opening of our third store in Yonkers, New York.

Aside from the logistics of building a new store, there were other questions that we had to face as well. Would our down-on-the-farm image work in New York? Could we compete against the many supermarkets, gourmet shops, and specialty shopping districts, such as nearby Arthur Avenue, that New Yorkers loved so much? Could we hire and train the kind of team that makes our stores fun places to shop?

The first step would be selecting the ideal person to be president of our new store. Stew and I both agreed to promote my nephew Tom Arthur, who had spent several years working for McDonald's and managing our Norwalk store for several years. Tom immediately began interviewing present Team Members in Norwalk and Danbury who volunteered to make the move to Yonkers. Tom's number one goal was to select only people who had proven that they were friendly and had a positive attitude. Tom knew well that this trait always outweighs skills or experience.

We assembled our new Yonkers management team, including Henry Gordon, who had worked his way up to meat manager in Norwalk and Danbury; John Talento, who had been a Norwalk produce department Team Leader and would manage the Yonkers produce department; and Ellen Story, a manager on our Norwalk human resources team. Tom and his team began to study the Norwalk and Danbury stores to decide the very best elements to include. The goal was to make Yonkers the best Stew Leonard's yet.

Tom and Ellen set up a trailer for Team members in the parking lot where we began taking applications and conducting interviews. We had won over customers in Connecticut with our "The Customer Is Always Right" policy. But here, many "big box" retailers had a totally different concept, with security guards posted at the store's exits, demanding to see the customers' sales receipts before they could leave the store. Would we be able to make our policies work in Yonkers? None of us knew for sure.

We would find out soon.

One day two women, Kathy Amdur and Lynne O'Brien, came in to interview for jobs in our meat department. They were best friends for life; they worked the same shifts, shared an apartment, and traveled to and from work together. Even though they'd been working at a grocery store for fifteen years, the store didn't offer them benefits. When they saw our Help Wanted sign on the hill above the New York Thruway, they came in to see Ellen. Acknowledging their enthusiasm, along with their experience and knowledge, not only in meat, but also in deli and grocery, Ellen wanted to hire them immediately. She introduced them to Henry Gordon, who explained the rules and expectations for working at Stew Leonard's: that respect for the customer is number one, that excellent quality is our top priority, that teamwork is essential in getting the job done. He went on to tell them of the benefits: health insurance, paid vacations, a 401(k) plan, company picnics, holiday celebrations, and appreciation dinners.

Kathy and Lynne later told us that they thought Henry was exaggerating. Ellen assured them that everything Henry had said was true, but they needed further convincing. Henry invited them to come up to Danbury and see how our meat department operates. They even had a chance to talk with several of our Team Members. They were wowed and immediately signed on.

We found that Kathy and Lynne were not alone in their skepticism about our dedication to the customer and our staff because most of the potential new Team Members also were, too. But just as with Kathy and Lynne, it wasn't hard to get our new Team Members quickly into the swing of doing things the Stew's way. We selected people who were eager for the opportunity to do a good job. They were proud to give good customer service, they loved creating excitement in the store, and they appreciated the good pay and benefits that came with the job.

As soon as each new Team Member was hired, he or she was sent to Danbury or Norwalk for training.

In September 1999, we threw a grand opening party on the covered plaza in front of the store. Since it was also Stew

Jr.'s forty-fifth birthday, we hosted a group of more than 500 people, including our new Team Members, the construction crews, many of our friends, and, of course, all our family. We set up a salad bar in the plaza, we grilled steaks and burgers, and onstage Little Anthony and the Imperials entertained the crowd. The guests were all invited to walk around the new store and see the changes and improvements that we made to our formula. We hosted Mayor Spencer, New York's Governor George Pataki, and other local dignitaries.

The next day when we opened our doors to the public, customers came pouring in—by the thousands. We were

At the grand opening of our Yonkers store, New York's Governor George Pataki joined the festivities.

overwhelmed, still getting our team in place, getting the systems and training right, and handling the unexpected large crowds. But everyone pitched in—Team Members and management working alongside each other wherever they were needed, bagging groceries, serving customers in the deli, collecting shopping carts. Some people were even getting their training right there on the floor, learning their jobs as they were helping customers

At first, we assumed that since Yonkers and southern Westchester County is a densely populated area, our customers would be mostly local. While our Norwalk store had long been a destination for customers who lived a good distance away, Danbury was more of a neighborhood store, serving local patrons who came in for something special like our custom-cut whole filet of beef as well as to pick up a half-gallon of milk. We thought Yonkers would be much the same. But to our surprise, Yonkers became a destination store as well. Nobody just happened to be driving by and said, "Oh, look. There's a food store. Let's go in and do our week's shopping," Instead, customers left home with their shopping lists, got onto the New York Thruway, and headed to Stew Leonard's. In fact, most customers pay a toll to get to us. People came from as far away as Upstate New York, Manhattan, and even Long Island.

Although our Yonkers customers liked our store, they also kept us on our toes. They were a very demanding group of shoppers. To many of them, meals were a sacred event for their families. And they were extremely sophisticated about food. They read cooking magazines, ate in the best restaurants in Manhattan, and kept up with the latest trends. They knew how Martha Stewart or Mario Batali prepared a dish, and they had an opinion on whether or not that was the right way to do it!

They knew exactly how they liked things: they wanted their steaks cut thick, just like the steakhouses cut them; they didn't want processed mozzarella, they wanted to see it being freshly made, right there in the store; they wanted to watch their sushi being rolled by hand. And everything they wanted was an opportunity for us: it was our chance to learn new things and to win over new customers. As we responded to our customers, they responded to us, becoming frequent and loyal shoppers. Within the first nine months, Yonkers was our top store.

One Hand Washes the Other

When we saw how well our customers in Yonkers responded to their own suggestions and ideas, we decided to implement those same ideas in our other stores. We expanded our meat departments, added dry-aged steak, set up sushi stations, and started making fresh mozzarella—and all were all huge successes! What had started as simply listening to the customer became sort of a sibling

Our Yonkers store, with its silo and barn-style building.

rivalry. When one store had a success, we implemented it in the other stores. Essentially, the team at each store worked not only to be better at what it did, but also to find things that would work in all our stores.

As a result, our new gourmet offerings became customer WOWs! Customers taught us how to improve our fresh-baked pizza, our handmade tortillas, our whole-grain breads, our kettle-fried potato chips, and our freshly made ice cream.

We heard about our Yonkers customers' concerns over antibiotics and hormones in meat. For years, we had insisted that there were no antibiotics or hormones in our milk. After talking to our cattle ranchers in Kansas, Stew Jr. found the perfect solution: we could create our own "all-natural" beef.

I am very fortunate that long ago Joe Shaw convinced me that we should simply use my own signature as our logo rather than design a fancy one. Joe believed that by doing so, I would be able to create a more personal image and give my customers the assurance that I personally stand behind everything in our store. That signature states our commitment to our customer and says: "All of us at Stew Leonard's really care!"

What I didn't realize then was that by using my signature and my name on the store, they wouldn't belong to me anymore. They would belong to everyone who worked there. They were our brand image.

I had always admired Frank Perdue for taking a commodity like chicken and turning it into a well-known brand with his own name. From the time I first met Frank, I dreamed that someday I might be able to emulate him and build a recognized and trusted brand out of my own little dairy store. But becoming a brand is much more difficult than just putting your name on the things you sell, more than doing things differently from your competition, more than being written about in Tom Peters's books or *People* magazine or *The New York Times*. Those things are why people will come

.o your store once. Your brand is why they come back again and again. It's the delivery on the promise of what you stand for, the experience that your customers have and their reaction. Our goal is to make our customers say WOW!, and when they do, they make our day. But all of that can't be accomplished by just one person. It takes everybody, working together to live up to the promise behind a brand-name company. As Tom Peters might say, "The brand image has to represent everyone's passion for excellence."

This secret was revealed to me the day that Frank Perdue checked the temperature in our coolers. His obsession with quality was what made Frank's brand stand apart. What he showed me was that attention to detail, above all else, is the magic in creating an excellent brand. We bent over backward to live up to that principle when we opened our store in Yonkers. In turn, we earned the customers' loyalty as our reward.

The actions and reactions of a member of our company directly reflect back on our brand image. A friend of mine, Patricia Fripp, a well-known motivational speaker and author, tells a story in her terrific book *Get What You Want* that really brings home the importance of how each team member's behavior can affect the image of the company he or she works for.

Early in the history of the Zellerbach Paper Company, a Zellerbach truck was following a rather fancy car along a narrow road. The truck driver was impatient to pass and kept honking his horn. After about fifteen minutes, when he finally did get an opportunity to pass, he stuck his head out of the window and yelled, "You jerk! You've been hogging the whole road." Then he roared off, the Zellerbach name all over the truck.

The gentleman driving the car was the owner of a company that just happened to be Zellerbach's best customer. When he returned to his office, furious, he ordered his purchasing agent to cancel all orders with Zellerbach and never to buy anything from them again.

It was several weeks before this lost account came to the attention to Mr. Zellerbach, but when it did, Mr. Zellerbach personally went to talk with the owner. When he heard about the truck incident, he apologized, but there was no way he could get the customer back again. His biggest account was lost forever, because one of his truck drivers had lost his temper and forgot that when he was driving the Zellerbach truck, he was Mr. Zellerbach!

It's the same at Stew Leonard's. I am not Stew Leonard anymore; everyone who works there is! Each and every one of our people represents the image of our brand, which stands for fresh products, friendly service, and above all, excellence in customer service. We must never forget it.

Building a brand of excellence doesn't stop with the design of a label, the development of a new recipe, or negotiating an amazing value on a popular item. We must all always continue to work hard at living up to our standards of freshness, value, and caring about our customers. By learning to strive for excellence in our business, our Team Members have

…ound that they have also learned to strive for excellence in their personal lives, helping many to achieve personal goals they thought they could never attain.

Their personal achievements in some cases have been quite amazing. Wendy Febbraio and Chris Arnette started as cashiers and are now human resource leaders, managing all the hiring and payroll activity for more than 2,000 people. Zita Sebastian started out packing cookies and bakery products at 2 a.m. Today, as director of fresh products for our entire company, she has more than 100 people reporting to her. She also earned an MBA. Our managing chef, Pierre Philitas, started out pushing shopping carts in the parking lot. He now supervises our Norwalk store's kitchen, with seven chefs and scores of staff preparing the tons of fresh products we sell each week. Ping Lu, who didn't speak any English when she arrived from China in 1990, worked her way up in our produce department, went on to help John Talento open the Yonkers produce department, and then became our Newington produce manager. Rich Lung, our art director, started off painting signs in Norwalk. He went to college to study art and came back to build up our very bustling art department. Roy Snider started out in 1980 packaging chicken and is now the manager of our Newington store and our companywide Director of WOW!

I know that it has not been easy for many of these people and that there have been constant struggles, but I love to praise their accomplishments because they have capitalized on the opportunities offered them. As someone who always believed that the best way to get people to do something is to get them to want to do it, it has been especially satisfying and rewarding to be able to help people rise to challenges and carve out career paths, and to watch them climb the ladder of success. It's been one of my own greatest joys to continually be reminded that as we are building our company, we are also building our people.

Life is strange with its twists and turns, and we never know what the future holds. When the state of Connecticut decided to build a highway right through the center of my dairy plant back in the late 1960s, I thought it was going to be the end of the world for my business. But it turned out to be a blessing in disguise. If the state hadn't forced us to move, there probably wouldn't be a Stew Leonard's business today. Through all of our struggles, we created a brand-new business, bigger and stronger than before.

The same thing can be said of my incarceration. It was caused by my dumb actions, for which there was a huge price to pay. I regret it deeply, but that difficult struggle was also responsible for making our family better and stronger. Those struggles forced me to transition our family business to the next generation, which in turn made us stronger.

For me; for Stew Jr., Tom, Beth and Jill; for my grandchildren; and for our Team Members, we all know that the secret of surviving struggles is attitude. When there is no choice, brave. And as Frederich Nietzsche said, “that which does not kill us makes us stronger.” Sometimes we learn more from failure than from success. The key is to extract the lessons so you never make the same mistake twice.

ACKNOWLEDGMENTS

There is an old Chinese proverbs that says, “When you drink the water don’t forget who helped you dig the well.”

I am grateful to my wife, Marianne, for her love, devotion, and support. She is my inspiration in everything I do.

Although they are no longer with us, I want to thank my friends Paul Newman, Frank Perdue, and Sam Walton, as well as Dale Carnegie. Each was instrumental in making this book possible.

I am grateful to my Mom and Dad for believing in me. At a very young age, I was groomed to run our family business because they believed in me. They will always be my heroes.

I am also grateful for my two brothers, Leo and Jim, who were always there for me and my four sisters, Helen, Marion,

Anna Lane, and Dorothy, who were also always at my side helping me through my challenges.

Bernie Gouz for sharing his common sense and wisdom. He pointed the way when I needed help.

My customers, many of whom I have served since I was a little boy, delivering milk to their homes, for your loyalty.

Our enthusiastic and hard-working Team Members, who do the heavy lifting at Stew Leonard's. Walt Disney once said, "You can dream, build, and create the most wonderful place in the world, but it takes people to make that dream come true." How true!

Dr. Léon Danco, Dr. John Ward, and Dr. John Davis for guiding our family through the rough spots of our family business and for their brilliant planning for our future.

Graeme Alford, my Australian friend and author, whose encouragement and enthusiasm never wavered. He constantly encouraged me to never give up.

Tom Peters put us on the map. His confidence and his belief in Stew Leonard's inspired us to achieve more than we could have ever dreamed possible.

Warden Dennis Luther for his belief and trust in me.

Scotty Reiss, my coauthor, deserves the credit for bringing this project to fruition. Scotty is the straw that stirred the drink. I am grateful for her dedication and hard work, but I am most appreciative for her persistence and empathy. She is very special. Scotty and her husband Craig were instrumental in making this book happen.

Marion Maneker, our publisher, and his talented team, whose guidance helped make this book a reality.

Rich Lung for his creativity and ingenuity.

It is impossible to thank everyone who helped me build Stew Leonard's into what it is today, but I'd like to acknowledge the following people: Mr. and Mrs. Thomas B. Stewart; Dominic, Bobby and Mickey Lametta; Charlie Miller; Christian Petersen; Walt and Gary Mislick; The Baylors; Bill Kolkmeyer; Barry Belardinelli; Patty Somma; Steve Guthman; Frank Guthman; Ray Flewellyn, Sr.; Ray Flewellyn, Jr.; Elaine, Tom, and Bruce Mathieson; Craig Hartmann; Shelly Gerardon; Ann Ainsworth; Nate Silverstein; Robert Schuller; Pastor Robert Brest, Woody Woodruff; Ray McMahon; Mort Perry; Hazel Schultze; Tom Flaherty; Frank Zullo; Dave Wilkes; and Lou Marcotte.

My deepest gratitude goes to our four children, Stew Jr., Tom, Beth, and Jill and their spouses, Kim, Karen, Bill, and Rocky for continuing to carry the torch.

And to our thirteen grandchildren, TJ, Blake, Emma, Sarah, Jennie Lynne, Jake, Britt, Will, Ryann, Chase, Andrew, Rex, and Madison: this book--and your place in this business--is my gift to you. As I look to the future, you WOW! me with your enthusiasm for the next generation of Stew Leonard's. It is my hope that this book will serve as an inspiration to you.

—STEW

When on a writing assignment for the *New York Times* in 2000, I discovered why I like Stew Leonard's so much—the passion, the dedication, the friendly people, and the great products. I figured there must be a book written about the celebrated man who created this company. To my surprise, there wasn't.

When I met Stew Leonard a few years later, I immediately saw that there was a book; it was in his head, waiting to be written. But since there were times in his life that he had no interest in reliving, and since he never wished to be seen as bragging about his accomplishments, he had never done it.

Stew politely told me that he wasn't interested in writing a book. But he left the door open: we exchanged email addresses and engaged in conversations that eventually became the foundation for writing his story.

Convincing Stew was one thing. Gathering my own enterprise was another. Without the support of my husband Craig, who believed in me from the very beginning, and my family, I don't think we could have accomplished what we have. Craig mentored me with his acute talent and experience in negotiating and conceptualizing, and also advised, edited, advocated, listened, and never once doubted my ability; to him I am forever grateful. My daughters, Cameron and Estee, who each take such great pride that I "work for Stew Leonard's," powered me on day after day; my mother Ann Williams, an accomplished author of historical books, and my father Jim, both of whom cheered me on; and my many, many family members and friends (including Caitlin

Reiss, Susie and Bob Frishman, Cory and Paola Kakol, Chip and Cheryl Skowron, Michele and Russ Turk, Jennifer and Michael Freitag, Terry Rogers, Reed Collyer, Amy Dixon, Polly and John Sanna) who have continually asked for updates on the project, each time renewing my enthusiasm for this story—Thank you!

I also want to thank Stew Leonard Jr., Beth Leonard Hollis and Tom Leonard, who each told me separately that I was probably wasting my time trying to get their father to write a book; he wasn't ready to talk about the difficult times in his life, they said. Then each turned to me and said almost exactly the same thing: 'I hope you can get him to do it! He's always wanted to write a book!' They each confided that they would love to see him achieve that dream.

I am especially grateful to Jill Leonard Tavello, who in her earnestness and genuine support for this project has given tremendous help, often in sorting out facts and stories and sometimes by just being the sane voice of reason. Thank you.

I owe a huge gratitude to Marianne Leonard who encouraged Stew, and me, to keep working at it. Her keen sense that this project could be not only the fulfillment of Stew's dream, but a priceless gift to her grandchildren was very often the inspiration we needed to keep going.

We are very lucky to have convinced Marion Maneker to work with us as our publisher. His experience, knowledge, and expertise enabled us to make our book a reality.

Of course, no project, especially one so colorfully painted

with the full range of emotions as the life of Stew Leonard, is a simple undertaking. There were many moments when I thought that this dream might, in the end, remain unrealized. So I am grateful to Stew for believing and trusting in me, and I am honored to have had the privilege to work so closely with him and to be infused with and inspired by his enthusiasm, his will, and his wisdom.

—SCOTTY REISS